Child Labour and Education

Child Labour and Education

By

Dr. M. Lakshmi Narasaiah
M.A., Ph.D.

Professor of Economics,
Co-ordinator, Department of M.B.A. and Commerce,
Special Officer,
Sri Krishnadevaraya University Post-graduate Centre,
Kurnool–518 002
Andhra Pradesh (India)

DISCOVERY PUBLISHING HOUSE
NEW DELHI

First Published - 2006

Reprinted - 2023

ISBN: 978-81-8356-064-1

Child Labour and Education

Published by:

DISCOVERY PUBLISHING HOUSE

4383/4B, Ansari Road, Darya Ganj
New Delhi-110 002 (India)
Phone: +91-11-23279245; 23253475; 43596065
+91 9811179893 / +91 9871656464
E-mail: discoverybooksindia@gmail.com
orderdphbooks@gmail.com
namitwasan9@gmail.com
web: www.discoverypublishinggroup.com

Printed at:
Infinity Imaging Systems
Delhi

Preface

In contrast to the food supply challenge posed by the coming wave of population growth, the global need for teachers and classrooms will rise very slowly in the next half-century. In many countries, the school-age population is increasing much less rapidly than the overall national population. The trend illustrates that growth rates typically differ for different age strata of the population. It has also shows that declining birth rates can take decades to move through an entire population.

At the global level, for example, total population is projected to increase by 54 per cent between 2000 and 2050, but the number of children aged 5 to 14 will grow by only 6 per cent. And of the world's largest countries-accounting for 60 per cent of global population in 1995—will actually begin to see decreases in the number of children aged 5 to 14 by 2015; for several of these countries, the decline in this age group has already begun. These countries will need fewer classrooms and teachers to educate the youngest members of society (assuming they maintain current class size and student-teacher ratios).

Plenty of nations, however, still have increasingly child-age populations. Where countries have not acted to stabilize population, the base of the national population pyramid continues to expand, and pressures on the educational system will be severe. In the world's 10 fastest-growing countries, for example, most of which are in Africa and the Middle East, the child-age population will increase in average 93 per cent over the next half-century. Africa as a whole will see its school-age population grow by 75 per cent through 2040.

The rapid growth in African populations is especially worrisome because of the extra burden it imposes in a region already lagging in education. Only 56 per cent of Africans south of the Sahara are literate, compared with 71 per cent for all developing countries. Few African countries have universal primary education, and secondary education reaches only 4-5 per cent of African children. Educating today's children is challenge enough; the addition of another three students for every four already there will require heroic investments in education. But the alternative is grim: without additional investments in education, today's average student-teacher ratio of 42 in Sub-Saharan Africa will reach 75 by 2040.

Many countries will be challenged to increase funding for education while ensuring that other worthy sectors also receive the support they need. With 900 million illiterate adults in the world, the case for a renewed commitment to education is easy to make. But competing for these funds are the 840 million chronically hungry and the 1.2 billion without access to a decent toilet.

The budget stresses on governments attempting to meet these basic needs would clearly be reduced with smaller populations. Mozambique and Lesotho, for example, both met the UNESCO benchmark for investment in education in 1992—6 per cent of gross domestic product—and the two countries economies were roughly equal in size. Yet because Mozambique has many times the population of Lesotho, spending per child in Lesotho is about nine times higher than in Mozambique. For the majority of countries who do not meet the UNESCO funding standard, many of whom also fall short in providing other basic services, a decline in population pressure could help substantially to meet all of their social goals.

If national education systems begin to stress life-long learning for a rapidly changing world, as recommended by a 1998 UNESCO report on education in the twenty-first century, then extensive provision for adult education will be necessary, affecting even those countries with shrinking childage populations, such a development means that countries that started population stabilisation programmes earliest will be in the best position to educate their entire citizenry.

Dr. M. Lakshmi Narasaiah

Contents

1

Stop Child Labour!

Although the internationally recommended minimum age for work is 15 years and the number of child workers under the age of 10 is far from negligible, almost all the date available on child labour concerns the 10 to 14 age group.

Traditionally, the proportion of working children has been much higher in rural than in urban areas—nine out of ten are engaged in agricultural or related activities. In the towns and cities of India where child labour has increased steadily as a result of the rapid urbanisation of recent years, working children are found mainly in trade and services and to a lesser extent in the manufacturing section.

Available statistics suggest that more boys than girls work. It should be borne in mind, however, that the number of working girls is often under estimated by statistical surveys, as they usually do not take into account full-time housework performed by many children, the vast majority of whom are girls, in order to enable their parents to go to work.

Girls, moreover, tend to work longer hours, on average, than do boys. This is especially true for the many girls employed as domestic workers, a type of emloyment in which hours of work are typically extremely long. This is also the case of girls employed in other types of jobs who, in addition to their professional activity, must help with the housework in their parents' home.

One of the factors affecting the supply of child labour is the high cost, in real terms, of obtaining an education. Many children work to cover the costs of school expenses. But, many schools serving the poor are of such abysmal quality or chances of upward mobility for graduates are so slim, that the expected return is not equal to the sacrifice made.... While it is true that many children drop out of school because they have to work. It is equally true that many become so discouraged by school that they prefer to work.

In manufacturing industries, children are most likely to be employed when their labour is less expensive or less troublesome than that of adults, when other labour is scarce, and when they are considered irreplaceable by reason of their size or perceived dexterity.

Many working children face significant threats to their health and safety. The majority are involved in farming and are routinely exposed to harsh climate, sharpened tools, heavy loads as well, increasingly, as to toxic chemicals and motorized equipment. Others, particularly girls working as domestic servants away from their homes, are frequent victims of physical, mental and sexual abuses which can have devastating consequences on their health.

Prostitution is another type of activity in which children, especially girls, are increasingly found. The AIDS epidemic is a contributing factor to this trend, as adults see the use of children for sexual purposes as the best means of preventing infection. The laissez-faire attitude of the authorities incharge of national and international tourism is also largely responsible for the current situation

Another extremely serious problem is child slavery in India. A large number of child slaves are to be found in agriculture, domestic help, the sex industry, the carpet and textile industries, quarrying and brickmaking. Child slavery predominates mainly where there are social systems based on the exploitation of poverty, such as debt bondage, when the motivation is the debt incurred by a family to meet a social or religious obligation or simply to acquire the means of survival.

There is a growing body of opinion that national and international efforts need to be more sharply focused on the most abusive and hazardous forms of child labour, granting them first concern and priority. Perhaps the most telling social argument against child labour is that its effects are highly discriminatory, adding to the burden and disadvantage of individuals and groups already among the socially excluded while benefiting those who are privileged. For that reason, child labour is inconsistent with democracy and social justice.

Action Required at the National Level

In the majority of states of India where child labour is common, the action taken until now to combat it has in no way been proportional to the extent and gravity of the problem. Many state governments have left it to economic growth and legislation alone to provide the solution. Experience has shown however that, unless specific measures are taken, growth in itself rarely benefits the very poor and that legislation means little where it is not vigorously enforced.

The problem of child labour will not be solved overnight. It is one of the many facets of poverty and underdevelopment. Resources available to reduce its extent and damaging effects are by definition scarcest in India that need them the most. Priorities must therefore be set.

No Effective Programmes Without Hard Information

Research: Almost everywhere, hard information is lacking on how many children are working, what they are doing, where and in which conditions. Without such data, it is virtually impossible to develop effective policies and programmes. Establishing, in some cases improving, data collection systems on child labour is an essential first step.

Raising awareness: A common attitude toward child labour in India is to accept it as an unavoidable consequence of poverty. Given the low quality and implied costs of the education services available to the poor, many parent, having themselves worked as children, tend to consider an early entry into the labour market, rather than schooling, as the best way to equip their children with skills useful for their future as adults.

Another difficulty is inherent in the fact that children working in rural areas, in urban informal sector workshops or as domestic servants in private households are not readily visible. An effective effort to protect children from workplace hazards or abuses must therefore begin by making the invisible visible. Experience clearly shows that significant public pressure is required to make progress on the child labour issue politically possible. As long as the general public, and in particular the middle and higher classes, consider that child labour is part of the harsh reality that makes good economic sense, the conditions for change will not be met.

The Government of India has restricted its role to enacting legislation, but has been passive in its enforcement. Most initiatives against child labour have traditionally come from Non-Government Organisations. In spite of their dedication however, their resources cannot be equal to the magnitude of the task. All levels of society need to do their share.

Some types of action can be provided only by the central government: child labour legislation and attendant enforcement mechanisms, the setting of public policy priorities and a publicly-funded system of basic education that offers quality schooling for all, including the children of the poorest families.

Trade Unions Bring Abuses to Light

Trade unions, are the logical leaders for bringing child labour abuses to light. They are ideally placed to document concrete cases of abusive child labour and to monitor the effectiveness of legal instruments and the performance of the labour inspectorate in the child labour field.

Employers and their organisations also have good reasons to be interested in the issue. Besides obvious humanitarian and social reasons, combating child labour makes perfect sense on economic and business grounds. Emotionally or physically damaged children have little chance of becoming productive adults.

NGOs' Strength is with Children Already Working

Like trade unions, NGOs can help to discover and publicize specific cases of abusive child labour. They are, in addition especially good at devising and implementing action programmes on behalf of children already in the labour market. Close to the children, they generally enjoy the trust of the local communities concerned and are well placed to appeal to their hearts and resources.

The participation of other segments of civil society—the media, universities, parliamentarians, teachers and educators—should be enlisted in the fight against child labour. All are valuable allies and can cooperate in complementary ways.

Establishing the required institutional capacity: To formulate and execute a national plan of action against child labour, institutional mechanisms must be established or strengthened within the governmental apparatus. These can then be entrusted with the responsibility for setting priorities, coordinating the activities of the various ministries concerned, promoting private sector participation and for launching and supporting pilot schemes to find new way of preventing child labour and of rehabilitating those who have been rescued from it.

Improving legislation and enforcement measures: In India legislation exempts from coverage precisely the kinds of wok in which children are most engaged (agriculture, family undertakings, small workshops, domestic service). A necessary first step to expanding protection under the law is to ensure that the main places where children work and the worst forms of child labour are encompassed by national legislation.

Improving schooling for the poor: The single most effective way to stem the flow of school-age children into abusive forms of employment or work is to extend and improve schooling so that it will attract and retain them. Recent trends however leave little room for optimism in that regard. In the eighties and early nineties resources devoted to education have dwindled steadily in India. The poor situation of the economy and the effects of structural adjustment policies were the reasons generally given for this decline.

Using economic incentives: As poor families need the income deriving from the employment of their children, it has often been considered appropriate to provide cash or in-kind payments as replacement.

Lively international debate over negative incentives: The advisability of using negative economic incentives has been the subject of much recent public debate. In Europe several department stores have decided not to sell products such as carpets unless they are certified to be made without child labour. Such movements by consumers and manufacturers alike have been accompanied by powerful efforts on the legislative and trade fronts as demonstrated by the hot debate on the incorporation of a social clause into international trade agreements. The United States has introduced conditionality into its Generalized System of Preferences, as has the European Union, to promote, among others, better labour standards and thereby discourage the use of child labour. A bill aiming at banning the import, into the United States, of goods produced by children (the Harkin Bill), has generated concern among employers and governments in countries heavily dependent on the United States for their exports.

There is no doubt that initiatives of this kind have helped significantly to raise public awareness about child labour. However, they have also had unintended consequences. The mere threat led employers of various industries to abruptly dismiss tens of thousands of children, the end result was that.

2

Child Labour in Weaving Industry

Approximately 1,30,000 children work in India's hand-knitted carpet industry. The working conditions are often poor, involving long hours sitting in one position, breathing cotton and wool fibres, eye-strain from doing very fine work and poor lighting. In the smallest enterprises the only light often available is the natural light filtering in through an open doorway.

Children are more likely to work in larger establishments: the smallest enterprises are family operations where the father and other family members might both weave carpets and till a plot of land, whereas the larger buisness use almost all hired labour. In the one-loom enterprises, approximately 14 per cent of weavers are children, while the number of a child labourers rises to around 33 per cent in businesses with five or more looms.

Although the proportion of child labour rises with the size of firm, the proportion does not rise as the quality of carpet increases; in fact, children are more likely to work on low-quality than on the highest-quality carpets. There is "no evidence that children dominate any particular design or quality niches". The opposite would be the case if the "nimble fingers" argument were true.

If the "nimble fingers" argument does not hold in the hand-knitted carpet industry, then it probably does not hold in other industries. Rejection of the "nimble fingers" argument is reinforced by the ability of adults to master carpet-weaving skills. Many adolescents and young adults who attend government training centres go on to run their own weaving businesses, while weavers say it takes a year to become fully proficient, whether one starts as an adult or a child.

Enterprises Often Small and Impoverished

The workforce of the hand-knitted carpet industry is mired in poverty. Most weaving enterprises in the Indian hand-knitted carpet industry are small, marginal operations run by poor and illiterate men, and they have no margin to pay higher wages. Most of the employers have never attended school; they began weaving before age 14. An enterprise normally consists of a loom set-up in a family's one-room cottage, with perhaps an additional loom, or looms, in an attached veranda or a shed. Male family members, including children, provide the bulk of the labour.

India's Factories Act has influenced the current structure of the carpet industry. Costly health, safety and labour regulations to which large firms are subject do not apply to cottage industries. Only a small proportion of establishment has five or more looms.

Competition Limits Retail Price Increases

While child and adult weavers have similar productivity, there is a cost advantage to hiring child labour: children earn less while apprentices than do fully-trained weavers, and their addition to the workforce depresses the going wage rate. Replacing the 22 per cent of children in the workforce would likely cause the wage bill to rise by about 5 per cent.

Given the small scale of many weaving enterprises and the fact that weaving charges make up approximately 40 per cent of the total production cost, with the loom owner receiving a fee equivalent to 10 per cent of production costs for supervision and provision of looms and premises, it is clear that the use of child labour can add greatly to the revenues and profits of loom owners.

The extra labour costs involved in eliminating child labour become much easier to absorb further down the distribution chain. Importing country wholesalers mark up the carpets around 65 per cent, while foreign retailers typically mark up the carpets by approximately 200 per cent. With sales or value-added tax, the carpets can easily cost four times as much to the consumer as the Indian export price. This means that the overall savings in production costs from the use of child labour are very small when compared to the foreign retail price.

Finding solutions which satisfy both local weavers and foreign retailers must avoid a beggar-thy-neighbour spiral. If carpet producing countries simultaneously implemented a no-child-labour strategy in their hand-knitted carpet industries, none of them would be at a competitive disadvantage.

Methods of reducing child labour such as those used in the garment industry where there is tripartite collaboration to ensure that the children are treated well and that there are educational opportunities for them until they are replaced without economic hardship to their families, is not likely to work in the hand-knitted carpet industry. Neither labeling nor inspection is likely to work here because the industry is too fragmented. It is impossible to control the thousands of cottages where one or two carpets per year are woven. We need solutions that address the general problems of poverty while developing alternative source of both employment and education.

Child labour is not necessary in the carpet industry. Children do not possess a unique skill and there is a ready pool of surplus adult labour ready to take over from them. "People should not be fooled into thinking that child labour is necessary for the industry to survive. The irreplaceable skills or "nimble fingers" argument should no longer be used to justify the use of child labour in the carpet industry or any other industry.

REFERENCES

Friedman, Milton and Kuznets, Simon, 1952. Income from Independent Professional Practice, National Bureau of Economic Research, Annual Series No. 45, New York, The Bureau.

Goldner, William, 1982. Labour Market Factors and Skill Differentials in Wage Rates, New York, The Association.

Levinson, Harold H. 1955. Wage Trends and Income Distribution, Michigan Business Studies 10, No. 4.

Lurif, Melvin, 1985. The Effects of Unionisation on Wages, Journal of Political Economy.

Garbarino, Joseph W. 1965. A Theory of Interindustry Wage Structure Variation, Quarterly Journal of Economics.

Ross, Arthur M. and Golden William, 1984. Forces Affecting the Interindustry Wage Structure, Quarterly Journal of Economic.

3

Child Labour

Targeting the Intolerable

We all know that child labour is one of the faces of poverty and that many efforts over many years will be required to eliminate it completely. But, there are some forms of child labour today which are intolerable by any standard. These deserve to be identified, exposed and eradicated without further delay.

The problem of child labour is so enormous and the need for action is urgent, choices must be made about where to concentrate available human and material resources. The most humane strategy must therefore be to focus scarce resources first on the most intolerable forms of child labour such as slavery, debt bondage child prostitution, work in hazardous occupations and industries, and the very young, especially girls.

In addition, a comparative study carried out over a period of 17 years in India on both children who attend school and children who instead work in agriculture, industry or the service sector showed that working children grow up shorter and weigh less than school children.

In Bombay, that health of children working in hotels, restaurants, construction and elsewhere was found to be considerably inferior to that of a control group of non-working school children. Working children exhibited symptoms of constant muscular, chest and abdominal pain, headaches, dizziness, respiratory infections, diarrhoea and worm infection.

Sexual Differences

Girls more often work as domestic labour, boys work in construction, fields and factories, leading to sexual differences in exposure to hazards. Girls, because of their employment in households, work longer hours than boys each day. This is one important reason why girls receive less schooling than boys. Girls are also more vulnerable than boys to sexual abuse and its consequences, such as social rejection, psychological trauma and unwanted motherhood. Boys, on the other hand, tend to suffer more injuries resulting from carrying weights too heavy for their age and stage of physical development. There are unsafe and abusive working situations for children. Some examples of these included:

Slavery and Forced Child Labour

Of all working children, those bound in slavery and forced child labour are the most imperiled. Children are still being sold outright for a sum of money. At other times, landlords buy child workers from their tenants, or labour "contractors" pay rural families in advance in order to take their children away to work in carpet-weaving, glass manufacturing or prostitution.

Prostitution and Trafficking of Children

The commercial sexual exploitation of children is on the rise, even though the subject has in recent years become as issue of global concern. Children are increasingly being bought and sold across national borders by organised networks.

Agriculture: Children work in agriculture throughout the world and often face hazards through exposure to biological and chemical agents. Children can be found mixing, loading and applying pesticides, fertilizers or herbicides, some of which are highly toxic and potentially carcinogenic. Pesticide exposure poses a considerably higher risk to children than to adults, and has been linked to an increased risk of cancer, neuropathy, neuro-behavioural effects and immune system abnormalities.

Mortality among child farm workers from pesticide poisoning is greater than from a combination of childhood diseases such as malaria, tetanus, diphtheria, polio and whooping cough. The operation of farm machinery by children also leads to many accidents which kill and maim.

Mining: Child labour is used in small-scale mines in many countries. Child miners work long hours without adequate protective equipment, clothing or training. They are also exposed to high humidity levels and extreme temperatures.

Mining hazards include exposure to harmful dusts, gasses and fumes that cause respiratory diseases that can develop into silicosis, pulmonary fibrosis, asbestosis and emphysema after some years of exposure. Child miners also suffer from physical strain, fatigue and musculoskeletal disorders, as well as serious injuries from falling objects. Children working in gold mines are endangered by mercury poisoning.

Ceramics and glass factory work: Child labour in these industries is common. Children often must carry molten loads of glass dragged from tank furnaces at a temperature of 1500-1800 degrees centigrade. They also work long hours in rooms with poor lighting and little or no ventilation. The temperature inside these factories, some of which operate only at night, ranges from 40 to 45 degrees centigrade. Floors are covered with broken glass and in many cases electric wires are exposed. The noise level from glass-pressing machines can be as high as 100 decibels or more, causing hearing impairment.

The main hazards in this industry are exposure to high temperatures leading to heat stress, cataracts, burns and lacerations; injuries from broken glass and flying glass particles; hearing impairment from noise; eye injuries and eye strain from poor lighting; and exposure to silica dust, lead and toxic fumes such as carbon monoxide and sulphur dioxide.

Matches and fireworks industry: Match production normally takes place in small cottage units or in small-scale village factories where the risk of fire and explosion is present at all times. Children as young as there are reported to work in match factories in unventilated rooms where they are exposed to dust, fumes, vapours and airborne concentrations of hazardous substances—asbestos, potassium chlorate, antimony trisulphide, amorphous red phosphorous mixed with sand or powdered glass and tetraphosphorous trisulphide. Intoxication and dermatitis from these substance are frequent.

Deep-sea fishing: In many Asian countries, children work in muro-ami fishing, which involves deep-sea diving without the use of protective equipment. The children beat on coral reefs to scare the fish into nets. Each fishing ship employs up to 300 boys between ages 10 and 15 recruited from poor neighbourhoods. Divers rest the nets several times a day, so that the children are often in the water for up to 12 hours. Dozens of children are killed or injured each year from drowning or from decompression sickness or fatal accidents from exposure to high atmospheric pressure, predatory fish such as sharks, barracudas, needle-fish and poisonous sea snakes also attack the children.

Child domestic workers: Children domestic service is a widespread practice in many developing countries, with employers in cities often recruiting children from rural villages through family, friends and contacts. Violence and sexual abuse are among the most serious and frightening hazards facing children at work, specially those in domestic service. Such abuse leads to permanent psychological and emotional damage.

Construction: Children undertaking heavy work, carrying massive loads and maintaining awkward body positions for a long time can develop deformation of the spinal column. Sometimes the pelvis can also be deformed because of excessive stress being placed on the bones before the epiphysis has fused. Children working in construction and other fields are exposed to other toxic and carcinogenic substances, including absebstos, one of the best known of human carcinogens.

One reason why modern societies and governments have not been more active in curbing the most harmful forms of child labour is that working children are often not readily visible. It is a matter of 'out of sight, out of mind'.

4

Children's Health and the Environment

Children today live in an environment vastly different from that of a few generations ago. Economic development, increased urbanisation and the consequences of war in many countries have added to the traditional environmental hazards, those problems associated with environmental pollution. Thus, while some traditional children' diseases such as diarrhea, malnutrition and infectious diseases persist in many countries, environmentally-related illnesses such as asthma, respiratory illnesses due to environmental tobacco smoke (ETS), as well as mortality and morbidity due to injuries, are increasing. In childhood cancer in some countries and the potential risks of endocrine-disrupting chemicals are among the emerging health threats that need careful vigilance. Children of lower socio-economic status are likely to suffer disproportionately from all these health threats as a consequence of living in highly polluted environments, poor quality housing, lower levels of education, and of restricted access to environmental and health care services.

Children's Vulnerability

The concern for children's vulnerability to environmental health threats is based on several factors. Children receive greater exposures than adults do because they drink more water, eat more food and have higher breathing rates per unit of body weight. Because they are undergoing rapid growth and development, toxicant effects at specific times may have irreversible consequences. For example, if vital connections between nerve cells fail to form during brain development, there is high risk that the resulting neurobehavioral dysfunction will be permanent and irreversible. Also, because most children have more future year of life than adults, they have more time to develop any chronic disease that may be triggered by early environmental exposures.

Public Health Threats

Asthma, injuries, and the effects of environmental tobacco smoke (ETS) are among the most significant public health threats to children. Childhood asthma is increasingly prevalent in almost all countries. What causes asthma is not known, but several environmental factors, such as indoor air quality (particularly exposure to the house-dust mite) and ETS, have been linked with the increase in asthma. In addition, outdoor air pollutants such as particulates; sulphur dioxide and ozone can exacerbate asthma symptoms. ETS, especially smoking by the mother, is a known risk factor for asthma. ETS is also known to cause acute and chronic middle ear disease and is associated with sudden infant death syndrome (SIDS).

Potential for Prevention

The variation in asthma and injury rates and the evidence of the role of certain environmental factors underline the potential for prevention. Public policies should seek to avoid preventable childhood diseases by preventing exposures to environmental agents and considering children's characteristics and susceptibilities in the development of environmental health legislation. Promoting citizen awareness and participation in policy-making through education and access to environmental information are important elements in achieving a safe environment for children. In this context, children are not only consumers with rights, but also citizens who can play an active role towards their own protection.

International Awareness

Several international agreements have acknowledged children's vulnerabilities and have committed their signatories to protect children's health from the effects of a deteriorating environment. This year, many countries will address several of the environmental health threats to children through international and national action. It is expected that a large international collaborative initiative will result under the guidance of WHO and other international organisation.

5

Helping Your Child Learn

A one-syllable word begins the education process: "Why?" Parents are always trying to answer that question. And that interaction between parent and child is the basis of much that children learn.

Teaching and learning are not mysteries that can happen only in school. They can also happen when parents and children do simple things together—things such as:

- Figure out whose socks are whose-sorting is a major function in maths and science.
- Cook a meal to learn science and good health.
- Tell each other a story as an important beginning for reading and writing; if the story is about the past, it's a way to interest a child in history.
- Plan a visit to a friend or relative for a personal connection with geography.
- Or play a game of hopscotch to develop counting and lifelong fitness.
- All children love their friends. So ask your child to describe his friend's appearance at the end of each school day. You can ask questions like. "What outfit did he/she wear?" or "How did he/she do his/her hair? This kind of routine query would encourage your child to observe his friend more minutely.

- If your child goes to school by bus, he can be asked to describe his route and point out certain landmarks namely colourful posters, traffic signals, large shops etc.

By doing things with their children, parents show that learning is fun and important—and that encourages children to study, learn, and stay in school.

Even on the discipline front, parents can help their children. Basic disciplinary principles must be tailored to each child and family. Before parents can become effective disciplinarians, they must first learn how to manage their own anger, solve problem situations and give and get support from others. Simple self-help techniques with or without professional support can help parents sharply reduce discipline problems.

Parents who are sensitive to their children's needs have more obedient children. Praise and love alone are not enough to instil good behaviour. Too much permissiveness hurts a child's efforts to develop self-control.

Behaviour problems should be reversed early. Waiting until the preteen-age years diminishes chances for success and puts children at higher risk for drug use and other problems.

Parents need to learn as many tricks of the trade as possible, including how to play with their children, communicate with them, praise and reward them and also set limits for them, as well as how to handle misbehaviour using a variety of techniques.

All that parents need to help their children is a willingness to observe and learn with them, and, to take the time to nurture their natural curiosity.

6

For a Broader Approach to Education

In our rapidly changing world, literacy should be seen as an important evolutionary variable in every society. For the further a society progresses, the more it needs to adjust and adapt to new demands and pressures, so that literacy is lifelong necessity for all.

Literacy, in the broad sense, is the foundation for life skills, ranging from basic oral and written communication to the ability to solve scientific and social problems. Today it involves much more than the acquisition of 3 Rs. And a limited set of traditional skills. It is linked with the changing demands of life in a given socio-cultural context.

This means that local communities should be fully involved in defining the content of literacy programmes. The local dimension of literacy is externally important, not only for accommodating the real needs of learners, but also for taking into account the linguistic and cultural realities of multicultural societies. For in the end, only the learners actually decide what they need to learn.

Building Bridges Between Cultures

Most literacy specialist have accepted this broader, more dynamic and culturally sensitive stance. It marks a long overdue acknowledgement of the positive role that local language and cultures can play in removing some of the serious pedagogical and psychological hurdles often encountered by learners, it is the only way to ensure the relevance and authority of literacy work.

Any one can insist here on the importance of multilingual education. Today education is as much about learning to live together as learning to know, to do and to be. Yet we cannot live together if our possibilities of expression are limited to a single linguistic frame. This is often at the root of problems encountered in multicultural societies. Of course, inequality in all its forms is a major factor. But internal conflicts often have purely cultural causes. It is more difficult for people to forge links with each other when they cannot communicate linguistically.

Yet children learn languages easily—much more so than the adults who take the decisions. We need to take much greater advantage of this fact. Children are expected to store too much information in their "hard memory"—much of it frankly useless! Giving them language skills provides them with bridges between cultures, enabling them to grow up without the debilitating sense that other cultures are lien. It is our task to try to ensure that education at all levels, and particularly basic education, promotes multilingualism. And we must invest in such education, since to do so is to invest in peace.

It is also important to remind ourselves that literacy is not a neutral process which can be applied in all situations, all the time, regardless of social and economic realities. Such a narrow concept of literacy ignores its critical role as a tool of empowerment. One can treat adult learners as empty vessels waiting to be filled with predetermined bodies of knowledge disconnected from their social experience. Literacy must provide space of intellectual development, motivations for learning and a sense of self-esteem, if it is to be a genuine education for empowerment.

Bringing Adult Education into the Mainstream

Many individuals and families around the world are facing unexpected changes in the pattern of their daily lives, disrupting their plans for the future. The demands on educational services are increasing dramatically, especially in countries where the state is the main provider of education for children and adults. In today's world, we cannot afford a short-sighted approach which, in effect, excludes adult education from the mainstream of the education system, even after the concept of life long learning has been accepted as a framework for educational policy.

Literacy programmes must be given the priority they deserve. Lifelong learning for all requires quality adult education and literacy programmes with qualified personnel, relevant teaching programmes, appropriate post-literacy materials and decent facilities. We must ask ourselves whether we recently are prepared to make the necessary. Investments in adult education and literacy to ensure universal access to the types of programmes needed to reach the targets of education for all.

If we truly believe in lifelong learning, and if we seriously believe in redressing the balance of learning in our societies, then we should seek to develop in every country an open and more enabling system of education, breaking with past concepts of education as something which happens to people between the ages of six and twenty and which only the privileged of few were entitled to. Synergy has to be created between formal and non-formal education programmes.

A case in point is the family literacy concept. We all know that the continuing education of parents, particularly when they are illiterate or under-educated, can contribute very effectively to their children's success in school. In fact the family literacy approach is one of the must effective ways of breaking the cycle of inter-generational illiteracy. Education and training policies should include all types of learning, whether it takes place in a school, in the workplace or at home. There should be more innovation and creativity in using methods and approaches.

7

Population Growth and Education

In contrast to the food supply challenge posed by the coming wave of population growth, the global need for teachers and classrooms will rise very slowly in the next half-century. In many countries, the school-age population is increasing much less rapidly than the overall national population. The trend illustrates that growth rates typically differ for different age strata of the population. It has also shows that declining birth rates can take decades to move through an entire population.

At the global level, for example, total population is projected to increase by 54 per cent between 2000 and 2050, but the number of children aged 5 to 14 will grow by only 6 per cent. And of the world's largest countries—accounting for 60 per cent of global population in 1995—will actually begin to see decreases in the number of children aged 5 to 14 by 2015; for several of these countries, the decline in this age group has already begun. These countries will need fewer classrooms and teachers to educate the youngest members of society (assuming they maintain current class size and student-teacher ratios).

Plenty of nations, however, still have increasingly child-age populations. Where countries have not acted to stabilize population, the base of the national population pyramid continues to expand, and pressures on the educational system will be severe. In the world's 10 fastest-growing countries, for example, most of which are in Africa and the

Middle East, the child-age population will increase in average 93 per cent over the next half-century. Africa as a whole will see its school-age population grow by 75 per cent through 2040.

The rapid growth in African populations is especially worrisome because of the extra burden it imposes in a region already lagging in education. Only 56 per cent of Africans south of the Sahara are literate, compared with 71 per cent for all developing countries. Few African countries have universal primary education, and secondary education reaches only 4-5 per cent of African children. Educating today's children is challenge enough; the addition of another three students for every four already there will require heroic investments in education. But the alternative is grim: without additional investments in education, today's average student-teacher ratio of 42 in Sub-Saharan Africa will reach 75 by 2040.

Many countries will be challenged to increase funding for education while ensuring that other worthy sectors also receive the support they need. With 900 million illiterate adults in the world, the case for a renewed commitment to education is easy to make. But competing for these funds are the 840 million chronically hungry and the 1.2 billion without access to a decent toilet.

The budget stresses on governments attempting to meet these basic needs would clearly be reduced with smaller populations. Mozambique and Lesotho, for example, both met the UNESCO benchmark for investment in education in 1992-6 per cent of gross domestic product—and the two countries economies were roughly equal in size. Yet because Mozambique has many times the population of Lesotho, spending per child in Lesotho is about nine times higher than in Mozambique. For the majority of countries who do not meet the UNESCO funding standard, many of whom also fall short in providing other basic services, a decline in population pressure could help substantially to meet all of their social goals.

If national education systems begin to stress life-long learning for a rapidly changing world, as recommended by a 1998 UNESCO report on education in the twenty-first century, then extensive provision for adult education will be necessary, affecting even those countries with shrinking childage populations. Such a development means that countries that started population stabilisation programmes earliest will be in the best position to educate their entire citizenry.

8

Will Education Go to Market?

The World Trade Organisation has launched processes that could open up to competition the expanding and highly protected world market in education. What issues are at stake? Most of us see education as first and foremost a public service which is responsible for providing young people with instruction. For investors looking for somewhere to put their money it is also an annual budget of $1,000 billion worldwide, a sector employing 50 million people, and above all a billion potential customers in the form of students.

The decision to extend services the liberalisation of international trade which previously applied to commodities was taken in 1994. The General Agreement on Trade in Services (GATS) which was signed in April of that year included education on the list of services to be liberalised. To say outside the scope of this agreement a country's education system must be completely financed and administered by the state, which is no longer the case anywhere. However, each country can still decide freely what commitments it wants to make, and especially which educational sectors it wants to expose to market forces. The New Zealand government, for example, has decided to open up to outside competition the whole private education sector, from primary to university level.

So far, New Zealand is an exception, but that situation is likely to change. Part 4 of the GATS agreement

("Progressive liberalisation") requires that fresh negotiations should be held by the end of 2000 at the latest, and should be directed to "the elimination of the adverse effects on trade in services of measures as a means of providing effective market access". At the Geneva headquarters of the World Trade Organisation (WTO), far from the headlines and the demonstrators, work still goes on. But independently of the WTO and national policies, a number of factors are driving educational systems towards "communication".

Pressures for Change

First, education is a rapidly-growing sector in which governments are finding it harder and harder to satisfy demand, above all in higher education. Between 1985 and 1992, the number of students in higher education rose about 26 per cent—from 58.6 to 73.7 million. Meanwhile, public spending on education has tended to stagnate over the past 15 years (5-6 per cent of GDP in rich countries and 4 per cent else where).

In view of this dearth of public spending, parents and students are increasingly looking to private education for a solution. In the United States, every episode of violence in a state school and every scandal that rocks official school systems gives a boost to "home schooling", where children no longer attend school and are taught at home.

Traditional public education is also coming in for strong criticism. Employers complain it is not geared to their needs and is not flexible enough. Under pressure from economic interests, a process of "deregulating" education system has begun. The growing independence of schools is encouraging them to look for alternative sources of funding, ranging from sponsorship to full management by private companies and including many kinds of partnerships between schools and firms. The time for out-of-school education has come... the liberalisation of the educational process thereby made possible will lead to control by education service providers who are more innovative than the traditional structures.

The development and spread of information and communication technologies on a massive scale make possible the development of paid distance learning, using multimedia and the Internet for tutorials, examinations, etc.

Secondary and primary education are also affected. More and more paying Internet sites bill themselves as alternatives to state schools or traditional private schools. The computer screen takes over from the teacher, for a fee of around $2,250 a year.

The WTO secretariat set up a working group in 1998 to look at prospectus for more liberalised education. Its report pointed to the rapid growth of distance learning and noted the increasing number of partnerships between educational institutions and private firms.

Education for Export

Some 350 U.S. experts on international trade in services, including 170 businessmen and women, gathered at the U.S. Commerce Department in Washington on October 16, 1998 to draw up recommendations for the U.S. negotiators at the WTO. The purpose of the meeting, called Services 2000, was to look at how the U.S. government should continue to support the efforts of American business to take competitive advantage in foreign markets. The US currently controls about 16 per cent of the world market in services. Its services exports have more than doubled in the past 10 years and now cover 42 per cent of the non-services trade deficit.

The United States is also the world's leading exporter of educational services, and a working group at the Services 2000 conference paid special attention to this sector. It concluded that the sector "needs the same degree of transparency, transferability and interchangeability, mutual recognition, and freedom from undue regulation or restraints and barriers that the United States acknowledges on behalf of other service industries". The report said that three points should be at the centre of WTO negotiations about education.

Firstly, there should be a free flow of electronic information and means of communication, nationally and internationally. Secondly, the negotiators should tackle "barriers and other restrictions that limit or prevent the provision of educational and training services across countries and internationally." They were also to deal with obstacles to the transferability of degree and diplomas.

Fighting for Market Share

The U.S. demands are backed by most countries of the APEC (Asia-Pacific Economic Cooperation) zone. In a note in October 1999, the Australian delegation to the WTO said it would be "encouraging all members to make expanded commitments in all sectors, even the ones that have proved difficult in both regional and multilateral services negotiations", particularly education.

South Korea took a similar position. At a meeting of Ministers of Human Resources from APEC Countries that it hosted in September 1997, the Seoul government put out a memorandum which clearly stated its vision of education as a tool of economic competition.

"The emphasis on education for itself or on education for good members of a community without a large emphasis on preparation for future work is no longer appropriate. Such a view of education and work cannot be justified in a world where economic development is emphasised.

"At present, in many economies, the education system do not sufficiently reflect labour market conditions. Their inflexible and inefficient education systems could not meet the new economic environmental challenges." So education should be made more "flexible", i.e. be deregulated and liberalised. In particular, "School systems should be established to allow all students to study what they are interested in "and "employers, with school educators, should share the role of educating students".

Some think resistance to liberalizing education will come from Europe, especially France. "The future WTO negotiations cannot call in question France's tradition of public service in the field of education and health", stressed a report on the WTO.

9

Private Education

The Poor's Best Chance?

Across the developing world, private schools and education companies are not only flourishing, but reaching the poor. India is a case in point. A Common assumption about the private sector in education is that it caters only to the elite, and that its promotion only serves to exacerbate inequality. On the contrary recent research points in the opposite direction. If we want to help some of the most disadvantages groups in society, then encouraging deeper private sector involvements is likely to be the best way forward.

Several developments are underway in India, all of which involve the private education sector meeting the needs of the poor in distinct ways. But India is not unique in this respect—similar phenomena are happening all over the developing world.

As a point of departure, how do government schools serve the poor? Usefully, the government sponsored Public Report on Basic Education in India (PROBE) from 1999 paints a very bleak picture of the "malfunctioning" of government schools for the poor. When researchers called unannounced on their random sample of schools, only 53 per cent had any "teaching activity' going on. In 33 per cent, the head teacher was absent. Alarmingly, the team noted that the deterioration of teaching standards was not to do with disempowered teachers, but instead could be ascribed to "plain negligence." They noted "several cases of irresponsible teachers keeping a school closed....for months at a time," many cases of drunk teachers, and head teachers who asked children to do domestic chores. Significantly, the low level of teaching activity occurred even in those schools with relative good infrastructure, teaching aids and pupil-teacher ratios.

But is there any alternative to these schools? Surely no-one else can do better than government given the resources available? As it happens, the PROBE report were serving the poor and conceded—rather reluctantly—such problems were not found in these schools. In the great majority of private schools—again visited unannounced and at random—there "was feverish classroom activity." Most parents would prefer to send their children to private schools if they could afford them. Private schools, they said, were successful because they were more accountable: "the teachers are accountable to the manager (who can fire them), and, through him or her, to the parents (who can withdraw their children)." Such accountability was not present in the government schools, and "this contrast is perceived with crystal clarity by the vast majority of parents".

The Way Forward: Loosen Regulations and Set up Voucher Schemes

To many readers, the existence of these private schools for the poor will come as a surprise. It was to me too, until I had the privilege of conducting field work for the International Finance Corporation (the private finance arm of the World Bank) on a group of such schools operating under the banner of the Federation of Private Schools' management based in Hyderabad, the federation has 500 private schools (from kindergarten to grade ten) serving poor communities in slums and villages. I was impressed by both the entrepreneurial spirit within these schools—they were run on commercial principles, not dependent on hand-outs from state or philanthropy—but also by the spirit of dedication within the schools for the poor communities served: not for nothing were the leaders of the schools known as "social workers". But these schools suffer under restrictive and inappropriate regulations. One example will suffice: to be recognised a school must deposit upto 50,000 rupees (about $1.200) in a stipulated bank account, of which neither the capital nor the interest can be touched. Given that the fees charged in these schools ranged from 25 (60 cents) to Rs. 150 per month (about $3.50) with most of the schools grouped near the lower end of the range, such sums are completely prohibitive.

Fees of around $10 per year are not affordable by everyone, but they are to a large number of poor families. Furthermore, the great majority of the schools offer a significant number of free places—up to 20 per cent—for the poorest students, allocated on the basis of claims of need checked informally in the community.

All of this suggests that if one is interested in serving the needs of the poor in India, then trying to reform the totally inadequate, cumbersome and unaccountable government system is unlikely to be the best way. Instead, reform the regulatory environment to make it suitable for the flourishing of private schools for the poor, help build private financing schemes using overseas and indigenous philanthropy, and encourage public voucher schemes so that parents can use their allowance of funding where they see the schools are performing well, rather than wasting them in unresponsive state schools.

Private education in developing countries isn't just about the poor, of course, and there are many exciting examples of big education businesses. But these too have implications for the ways in which the private sector can reach the least advantaged. One Indian company which embodies much of the excite the National Institute for Information Technology (NIIT). With its competitor, Aptech, it shares just over 70 per cent of the information technology education and training market in India estimated at roughly Rs. 1.1 billion ($24 million). NIIT has 40 wholly owned centres in the metropolitan areas, and about 1,000 franchised centres across India. It also has a global reach, with centres in the U.S., Asian Pacific, Europe, Japan, Central Asia and Africa. A key aspect of NIIT's educational philosophy is that there is a need to harness research to improve the efficiency of learning and to raise educational standards.

Because of its success in developing innovative and cost-effective IT education and training, NIIT has attracted the attention of several state governments. First off the mark was Tamil Nadu, which wanted to bring a computer curriculum to all of its high schools. Significantly, although allocating about $22 million over five years to this endeavour, it didn't hand the funds over to government schools, perhaps in light of the PROBE report's lessons. Instead, it developed a model to contract out the service to private companies, which provide the software and hardware, while the government supplies electricity and the classroom. For the first round of the Tamil Nadu process, 43 contracts were awarded for 666 schools, with NIIT allotted 371 schools. Many of the classrooms have become NIIT centre, open to school children and teachers I daytime, then used by the franchise holder in the evenings. The contracting out of curriculum areas such as this represents an important step forward in relationships between the public and private sectors, and provides an interesting model worth watching and emulating.

Most recently, NIIT has focused on reaching largely illiterate and unschooled children through the Internet. Within weeks of having set up an "Internet kiosk" in a slum area, the institute's researchers found that without any instruction, children could achieve a remarkable level of computer literacy. NIIT is exploring ways to roll out the idea commercially, harnessing the power of the private sector to reach the poorest through modern technology.

These initiatives all find echoes in other developing countries. In each case, the private, not the public sector, is most responsive to the needs of the poor, and is brining innovation, efficiency and educational quality to the lives of the most disadvantaged. The private sector has the potential to promote greater equity and to influence education policy, provided it is encouraged and viewed as a partner, not a threat to governments, whether in the developing or the developed world.

10

Corporate Ambitions in Education

Centralisation and efficiency, frequently invoking the powerful metaphor of scientific management or "Taylorism," using the stopwatch and management to discover the "one best way." These principles had been instrumental, industrialists of the time believed, in creating the industrial revolution and the wealth of powerful international companies. The quest for efficiency of those decades led to the problems we must now repair, notably the rigid and bureaucratic structure of our school systems.

Today, public schools continue to adapt new business efficiency techniques in what seems to be a constant recycling process. Scientific management, it turns out, was only the precursor to a host of ever newer management theories aimed at encouraging greater worker productivity and hence greater national wealth.

When Schools Become Levers to Attract Business Investment

These trends have echoes in the management reforms prescribed for and adopted by schools. Some seek increased efficiency through decentralised school governance while others image that outsourcing (or contracting) the management and operation of schools will lift educators' performance because incentives are lacking in secure government jobs.

All this is happening against the backdrop of economic globalisation, which inevitably creates political tensions by pitting governments against one another in competition for transnational corporate jobs and global capital. Our current era mimics the turn of the century to the extent that international capital flows and transnational production processes influence both corporation and governments. Today, technologically induced speed, growth among investors, concentration of wealth, and interconnectedness have increased the effects of this global speculation and decreased the capacity of governments to regulate business and markets. Not surprisingly, this global market ideology has been broadly recognised as a force in national education policy.

Reforming local schools becomes one of the ways that cities engage in the global competition to provide production resources to corporations. When formal schooling is seen as a key element of productive capacity, a view reinforced by the decline of manufacturing and the rise of information-based technologies, the quality of the local public school system takes on renewed importance for business leaders and local politicians alike. Today's corporate leaders have uncommon access to elect political officials and government agency heads, the wealth of large corporations to draw upon, and the ability to affect local and regional economics simply by making business decisions.

Schools are treated as engines of economic development to lure business to a particular city or state, so corporate and local political leaders cooperate in their governance and redesign. In short, school policy becomes labour policy?

This powerful combination of corporate, national and state executives is happening at the expenses of education professionals. In contrast to the turn of the century, when educators played a pivotal role in debates by emphasising the role of schools in developing citizenship, today they have been largely discredited. Selecting school leaders from outside the field has become both symptom and spur to this decrease in the educator's status. A small but influential group of school districts is choosing leaders from among the ranks of businessmen, politicians and the military, rather than educators.

All this is taking place with little evidence that recent management solutions will turn around poor schools, nor that improvements in school performance protect against declines in productivity or the business cycle. Yet there are more troubling problems with reform strategies that pit the market against government in education. One is that education is reduced to its narrowest economic purposes. According to a 1992 survey, corporate executives most want schools to emphasize "a basic understanding of math and science:" and "sound work habits such as self-discipline, timeliness and dedication to work." These are laudable goals, but reflect a narrow set of traits that employers predict their workers will need in an information economy.

The corporate model of reform pays little heed to other expectations of public schools: building just and tolerant communities, reducing distrust of one another and our shared institutions, safe guarding democratic ethics and introducing children to the cultural wisdom of the world. We are also witnessing the abandonment of many kinds of equality. Neither markets nor business ethics routinely put equality or fairness above profits. Whole groups of people will not fit the prevailing model of what it takes to be competitive in an educational market place in which competition is the guiding principle of improvement. Another disturbing trend is the anaemic citizenship that economic justifications for schooling envision. Increasing the emphasis on individualism is likely to exacerbate a pattern of civic disengagement many already find disturbing in its scale and scope.

A Balancing Act to Reach a Healthy Equilibrium

We need a contemporary counter-movement to restore a healthy equilibrium of goals for our public schools. This movement would be grounded in a very different educational critique that rejects the metaphor of market (or management) failure and instead tackles the problems in our schools as symptoms of a widespread civic breakdown. The solutions to school failure would then hinge on common concerns, rather than rigorous individual competition and accountability. In addition to academic criteria parents and reformers would craft student performance measures that reward active citizenship, tolerant and respectful behaviour, and cultural knowledge in the arts, history and languages. This reform movement, seeking equity and tolerance, would revitalize democratic institutions and not merely aim for more efficient production.

11

Promotion of Higher Education in Research

The central role of Universities in the development of skills and knowledge as an absolute prerequisite for national development is un-disputed. Higher education institutions have the responsibility for training a country's high level professional, technical and managerial personnel, they are to generate new knowledge through research and advanced scientific training, and they serve as agents in the transfer, adaptation and dissemination of knowledge. Higher education institutions also play an important role in contributing to the social cohesiveness of a nation and as a forum for constructive debates on development.

In a world economy which is heavily science-based and technology-driven higher education institutions, and particularly universities, have to provide such a competence which is indispensable for building a country's endogenous capacity for problem identification and problem solution through education combined with research. In India, however, universities have so far not been able to fulfill these roles, partly because the multiplicity of their missions is hardly compatible. Many critics of the universities in India consider them to be institutions of learning and research separated from the main stream of the economic and social needs of the population which they are supposed to serve. Most of them have not managed to reconcile the missions of providing country-oriented training and research and of being part of a wider international scientific community. Higher education institutions in many countries all over the world are confronted with a large scale and mostly uncontrolled expansion of the higher education sector and the concomitant growth expenditure against a background of dwindling financial resources to support such expansion. As a result of this expansion the quality of teaching and research has declined due to overcrowding, inadequate staffing, poor physical facilities and equipment. In addition universities often show a poor capacity for management and administration. This results in a low internal efficiency which amongst others is responsible for a rising graduate under or unemployment.

These deficiencies and a lack of national resources produce dependence on external sources particularly for research development. The low capacity for planning and management makes it difficult to properly employ external sources so that there may be pockets of good quality research in one field unrelated to neighbouring areas and not forming part of an endogenous research tradition.

Measures to be Taken

The measures may be aimed specifically at increasing the efficiency of the system of higher education or of individual institutions by improving development relevance, quality and performance. More specifically are:

- to optimise and diversify the structure in line with the country's development requirements;
- to improve the capacity for efficient planning and administration;
- to diversify funding sources, with the aim of relieving the state budget;
- to improve access for talented students from all segments of society, giving special attention to the proportion of women studying.

At the level of individual institutions of higher education the aim should be improve

- education and training performance in the academic-scientific and vocational field,
- research and development capacities, especially in applied fields;
- the capacities to provide constancy and services to contractors in state, business and industry, and society.

In order to achieve these objectives, it is necessary

- to train the academic, administrative and technical staff,
- to improve the infrastructure including central facilities and means of communications, and
- to increase efficiency by improving organisation.

The concept stresses the importance of measures designed to increase the efficiency of higher education in general through the strengthening of management capacities both at the system and at the institutions levels. This extends, inter alia, to the diversification of institutions of higher education in line with development needs, diversification in terms of funding (including cost sharing through fees) diversification in terms of study courses and practice-oriented training offered. Academic training at different levels for technical and executive staff.

New Areas of Promotion

The promotion of higher education institutions and subjects considered relevant for development (agriculture, natural sciences, engineering, medicine), the revised concept has to include areas such as the protection of the environment and resources, education, family planning and population policy.

In the wake of the political and economic reorientation taking place in many countries subjects like economics, law and social sciences are increasing in importance.

Prospects

Each country needs capacities which can produce the

necessary analytical competence and research for generating information needed for designing and monitoring its development path. Institutions of higher education are essential in providing this competence. The responsibility for advanced education and the production of ideas and information should not be left to external donors. This may entail the concentration of resources, both internal and external, on one or only a few institutions of a country.

12

Wanted

An New Deal for the Universities

Higher education must meet new demands in order to turn out well-trained professionals instead of unemployed graduate. We are living through a period of profound historical change, marked by an on-going knowledge revolution. Society is changing far more quickly than the structures it has created and the quickly than the structures it has created and the universities are lagging behind these changes. They, and the educational system in general, continue to teach the use of static processes, forecasting models based on historical experience and the memorizing of solutions to already solved problems.

Higher education systems in both North and South are in crisis, both quantitatively and qualitatively. Naturally the developing countries are the hardest hit, both in terms of available resources and levels of student enrollment.

Is the crisis due to a shortage of funds alone? Does the fact that the countries of the North invest ten times more per student than those of the South mean that graduates from the former are ten times better trained? Common sense says yes. But in most cases the answer is no. Generally speaking, university education has failings all over the world, in some cases because it is an offspring of a wasteful society, indifferent to the resources with which that society provides them.

The Missing Link between Education and the World of Work

In the United States, for example, many teachers and researches come from developing societies which should theoretically have given them a less sound training than that provided by the immense academic and financial resources of the United States system. But this is not the case: they compete professionally and scientifically, with no major problems. In many areas the results of university training are comparable.

Professionals move around because they need jobs and want to work in the best possible working conditions. There are, for example, almost 30,000 African Ph.Ds working in Europe and North America, and thousands of Latin American and Asian professionals working in the Untied States. By the beginning of the 1990s about a million professionals had emigrated to the developed countries over the previous three decades, and the figure has increased considerably in the last five years. While the number of opportunities and access to them are uneven, there is little difference between North and South as regards quality; nor is the availability of funding the only basis for improving the system.

The problem is that post-secondary training today is diploma-driven. It is based on rigid study programmes and is changing at a rate which takes little or no account of the speed of knowledge accumulation. This is despite the fact that today's graduate professional needs to have followed a flexible curriculum and must be a problem solver, extremely adaptable to new processes and technologies, generously endowed with creativity and firmly inclined towards lifelong learning, as is clear from the studies on skilled labour done by industrialized countries and from numerous OECD studies.

A recent study of the relationship between higher education and the labour market observes that there appears to be no connexion between the increase in professionals' level of knowledge and changes on the labour market. Although the market undoubtedly demands basic skills and knowledge, it is attaching increasing importance to the emotional and psychological attitudes of future employees.

Although post-secondary education is clearly associated with higher personal incomes, lower unemployment and greater opportunities to climb the social ladder, unemployment rates for people with higher education qualifications continue to be high in both North and South. Graduates unemployment in Europe, for example, varies between 1.4 per cent and 16.6 per cent depending on the country. What's more, many graduates are working in jobs outside their field of training. The increase in graduate unemployment in the developing countries is largely due to the drastic fall in demand from the major employer of graduates—the state—as a result of international competition and new political and economic approaches. The private sector is in no position to absorb the supply of surplus graduates. World Bank studies carried out in Asia, the Middle East, North Africa and certain Latin American countries show that graduate employment is increasing.

All the same, higher education cannot be held wholly responsible for graduate unemployment nor for the correlation that should exist between training, study programmes and demand for labour. It is often said that higher education is failing to provide training in the activities required by the market, but the market is often incapable of adequately anticipating the type of professionals it is going to need.

A survey conducted in Florida (USA) among multinationals in the high-tech and services sectors reveled companies that were unable to identify the professional qualities that would be required within ten years and, in many cases, within five years. This is not surprising, in view of the spectacular rise of the Internet between 1994 and 1998 which caught many hardware and software firms unawares. It is in information technology that redundancies and high unemployment levels are occurring, because systems are constantly changing and because of strategic mergers between the major companies.

Another example of the difficulty of making reliable predictions concerns those made by the European Community and the US Government regarding the type of jobs that would be needed at the beginning of the new century. These predictions were inaccurate: what had been forecast to occur after 2001 actually came about in the late 1980s and early 1990s.

It can be said, however, that professional training over the come years will focus on areas such as high-tech electronics, information technology, aqua-culture, agro-energy, biotechnology and energy physics. Jobs in information and communication systems will require new qualifications which will have to be continually updated. The service sector will experience spectacular growth in the field of leisure and recreation because of the reduction in working hours. New professions in the human sciences such as "ludicadology", incorporating psychology, pedagogy, information science and the technology of education, play and creativity programmes, will replace the old single-discipline approach.

In short, the great occupational change looming ahead will call for increased interdisciplinary, revitalisation of the disciplines related to thick and aesthetics and sweeping changes in the attitudes of teachers and students: for the professional of the future, education will be a lifelong process, and education and work will go hand in hand.

The great challenge will thus be to create a stable relationship between higher education and society through strategic alliances with the production system designed to promote participation by all sectors of the economy in the university's basic and applied research programmes and by production-sector specialists in university teaching.

The problems of the university are also those of society, and so are the responsibilities. This rises the question of the university's specific culture, especially the teacher-student relationship. Planning is currently based above all on the teaching staff, which is more corporatist than academic. Physical spaces, salary scales, curricula, structures and timetables are more closely geared to the needs of the teacher than of teaching. This is the case all over the world.

More serious still, this teacher-centred culture is giving way to one that is even more dangerous for the survival of university education: an administration-centred culture. This would mean an education system dominated by bureaucrats and the kind of management structures which would place an institution whose function is to produce and disseminate knowledge on the same footing as a detergent factory or a multinational travel agency.

But no strategy for change can work unless higher education adapts to the challenge of the knowledge explosion. It is vital that course content should be geared to what learners "must know" and not to what teachers "know" or "think they know". This will force teachers into a permanent renal of theories, techniques and processes, keeping up with knowledge produced both inside and outside the university. Higher education is evolving towards a model in which lecturers and students will be permanent learners and where curricula will be drawn up on the basis of innovation, fresh knowledge and the latest teaching and learning technologies. Above all the university must teach people to think to use common sense and to give free rein to the creative imagination.

13

Wiring up the Ivory Towers

Prestigious universities are forging alliances to conquer a share of the e-learning market and stand up to virtual competitors. Just like airline companies, universities around the world are forming partnerships and consortia in response to the pressures of globalisation. The World Education Market held in Vancouver was a timely sign: the fair, expressly organised to foster relations between universities, training providers, software companies and representatives from nations with large education needs attracted participants from over 60 countries.

This race to "partner up" is fuelled by a number of factors. In most industrialised countries, government funding for higher education has decreased, forcing institutions to look for new markets either to subsidize campus programmes or just to remain viable. There is a growing need for lifelong learning as "jobs for life" vanish and the information society drastically reduces the shelf-life of almost any educational qualification. Technological developments, increasingly necessary for learners in all fields to master, offer ever more innovative tools for supporting e-learning.

For business, online learning is "the" new market opportunity with the need for re-training and professional updating predicted to increase an $11.5 billion industry by 2003. Business is better able to develop and maintain the technological infrastructure necessary to run large online systems and everyone, including the universities, recognizes that it takes robust telecommunications technology to deliver education and training on the scale demanded.

A host of companies has sprung up to help universities shape and package courses for online presentation, while network providers are jockeying for position to deliver online education.

The United States is the undisputed leader in the field, prompting governments in the U.K., Canada and Australia to commission being eroded by U.S. ventures turned global Canada and the U.K. are in the early stages of setting up their own virtual universities. But what has become clear is that the conservative and labyrinthine decision-making processes which characterize most university procedures are being jolted by a race to get a share of the lifelong learning market.

So far, the most common approach for universities to break into the e-learning universe has been to develop courses specifically for a corporate partner or to form alliances among themselves. Universities 21, a company incorporated in the U.K. is a network of 18 leading universities in ten countries.

Very often, prestigious universities has stayed clear of going fully online, seeing a danger to their brand name. Many are limiting their offerings to continuing education programmes and/or non-degree courses, and more often than not, they are aiming at the corporate market. One Company UNext.com, has partnered with first-class institutions such as the University of Columbia (U.S.) and the London School of Economics to create online courses marketed under the name Cardean University. Their target: the Fortune 500 companies as well as individual adults. They've managed to attract Noble laureates to design courses and the universities have formed spin-off for-profit companies specifically to develop online programmes. This facilities the commercialisation of software and other products, and is a way to take a commercial approach to continuing and professional studies without compromising the Univesity's standing.

Then there are the free-standing for profit virtual universities which are arousing the ire of institutions that have prided themselves on a long history of public service. The most quoted examplar is Phoenix University, the largest private outfit in the U.S. Now owned by the Apollo Group, it operates the country's largest online programme with 12,200 students. The university tracks students progress and contacts those who don't submit assignments on time or fail to enrol in subsequent courses. Many critics question Phoenix's blatant commercialisation, but few doubt the university's impact on continuing professional development provision.

Although e-learning is in its infancy, its impact can already by gauged. New providers are coming on the market all the time and the trend is accelerating to the point of upsetting universities virtual monopoly in educational accreditation. An Information Technology training course offered or accredited by Microsoft has undoubtedly become more valuable than a Bachelor of Science from a renowned university.

The more consumerist the approach of the education provider, the more what is taught is influenced by demand. MBAs dominate e-learning provision and IT courses are a close second. While the new consumer/learner demands flexibility, choice and just-in-time learning opportunities, suppliers will inevitably arise who are focused on meeting the demand at the expense of quality and value. And is the consumer really the best judge of what course material to choose? Education is a more complex "product" than toothpaste or washing powder. A totally consumer driven education market is unlikely to be in society's best interest in the long term. The commercialisation of education usually goes hand-in-hand with desegregation: course design, delivery, tutoring assessment and accreditation may be carried out by different organisations. Students might study courses or modules from different universities or providers and then put themselves forward for examination and accreditation by yet another institution. While most academics loathe marking assignments, they regard this scenario with horror, and blame commercialisation for the demise of the 'community of scholars' concept of a university. The death of the 'course' has also been predicted, with learners—especially corporate and on-the job learners—demanding short study modules. What then happens to the ability to get an overview of a field when learning consists of the students selecting a whole series of unconnected learning "bites"? Learners will be "zapping" between short sequences or presentations much as they do between television channels.

But while some faculty view e-learning with alarm, technology-based learning is where most of the pedagogical innovation is taking place in universities. Multimedia learning resources and interactive simulations are being developed for the web. Collaborative learning activities, new forms of online assessment and small group teaching technologies are making online courses more stimulating, interactive and attractive than many face-to-face taught courses.

Despite "doom and gloom scenarios", most moderate observers of the scene see a continued future for the campus university, especially at the undergraduate level, while e-learning will above all cater to adult professional and independent learners. Some commercialisation of education is good if it fosters innovation, concern for quality and responsiveness to consumer demands. But if some is good, more is not necessarily better! Not in education at least.

14

Shaking the Ivory Tower

Universities have changed radically to keep pace with modern life. No where are they heading in this high-speed age? In the past half century higher education has been transformed from a privilege conferred on social and political elites to a mass activity available to whole populations. This process began in the United States in the 1940s and 1950s, spread to most of Western Europe and many other developed countries during the 1960s and 1970s and in the past two decades has become a global phenomenon. In the next half century it will accelerate, leading perhaps to the replacement of "higher education" (still an elite-ish category despite its expansion) by extended systems of "lifelong learning".

The key to this transformation has been the expansion of secondary education. For example, in all but two countries of the OECD (Organisation for Economic Cooperation and Development) at least two thirds of young people now complete upper secondary education, and so are eligible to enter higher education. The result has been a dramatic increase in enrollment rates in higher education. In Chile the total number of students has grown from 131,000 in 1978 to 235,000 in 1988 and to 343,000 in the mid 1990s. Even in the United States, the pioneer of mass-access higher education where very high secondary education completion rates had already been achieved before 1970, the student population has continued to grow, from 11 million in 1978 to 13 million in 1988 and now to more than 14 million.

The forces have driven up completion rates in upper secondary education and enrollment rates in higher education. The first has been democratisation. As late as 1945 high levels of social, and hence educational, inequality persisted even in democratic countries, and much of the world remained in the grip of colonial and totalitarian powers. In North America, Western Europe and Australasia democratisation typically took the form of the development of "welfare states" in which there was an increase in public expenditure on education, housing, health and social security that was sustained over more than three decades after the end of the Second World War.

More recently, as renewed emphasis has been placed on the market even in social policy, the rise of consumerism has continued to fuel demands for increased higher education opportunities. The older idea of education as a civil entitlement has been compounded by newer notions of free access to the education marketplace. Far from arresting the advance to mass higher education, consumerism has accelerated it in most developed countries. As traditional forms of social differentiation based on class, gender and ethnic origin have been eroded by democratisation and by market forces, new forms based on educational certification have become more important. In many developed countries the middle class and the "graduate class" have tended to coalesce.

In much of Asia and Africa democratisation took the form of decolonisation. In newly independent countries the energy originally generated in liberation struggles against the colonial powers was directed into a wider struggle to create fairer and more equal successor societies. Education was central to this struggle. The result has been a rapid increase in higher education enrollment, for example, in Tunisia from barely 2,000 students at the time of independence to more than 100,000 today. That process continues.

However, the relationship between democratisation and the development of higher education has been less straightforward in developing countries. Despite very rapid rates of expansion the "metropolitan" influences of the former colonial powers have lingered more stubbornly in higher education than at other levels of education. This is partly due to the continued influence of associations between universities in the British Commonwealth as well as those between francophone universities.

Partly because of these lingering "metropolitan" models and partly because levels of participation are still lower than in developed countries, many African or Asian universities have remained more elite institutions than higher education institutions in North America and Europe. Also, as economic conditions have worsened in some developing countries, the competition between primary and higher education sharpened in the post-independence years as both were seen as equally important priorities. This competition was often reinforced by the intervention of the World Bank.

The second force driving up higher education enrollments has been the changing nature of the labour market. Traditional occupations have become comparatively less significant, while new service occupations, which often require graduate-level skills, have become more important.

Skill requirements have been become more sophisticated. Jobs once done by unskilled or semi-skilled workers are now undertaken by technicians; and those which as recently as the 1980s were taken by technicians are now likely to be filled by graduates. The capital invested for every worker has more than doubled in the past 20 years. Even in occupations where there is less evidence that skills contents have changed significantly, university graduates are now employed in much larger numbers, partly to enhance the social status of these occupations and partly to compete in a graduate-dominated labour market. Healthcare is a good example. Once doctors were the only graduates; today, many para-medical workers are also trained in higher education.

The second form taken by the economic driver has been the growing conviction that national success now depends on economic competitiveness which, in the context of a knowledge-based economy, depends in turn on an adequate supply of human capital. Knowledge is now seen as the key economic resource.

This analysis my be exaggerated; raw materials are still very important in national economies and the global economy. But it has become pervasive- and persuasive. The naïve and linear theories of human capital popular a generation ago which postulated a direct link between investment in education and economic growth may have been challenged; some forms of higher education are now as likely to be labelled consumption as investment goods. Nevertheless, the discourse of the "Knowledge Society" has become even more powerful.

The impact of democratisation and economic competitiveness on higher education has been immense. First, the expansion of student numbers has made the cost of higher education a significant element within national budgets for the first time. A number of important consequences has flowed from this—the opportunity, and incentive, to compare the value of investing in different levels of education; increasing demands that universities are run as efficiently as possible (compromising their traditional autonomy from the state—and the market); lower unit costs as budgets have been trimmed (which may have undermined higher education's claim to represent academic excellence). Second, higher education systems have emerged that embrace not only traditional universities but also non-university institutions. Two effects have been produced. One is that the ethos of the traditional university has been eroded; it no longer stands in glorious isolation. The other is that institutional differentiation has been encouraged, whether through active state planning or in response to markets for teaching and research.

The prospects for the next half century are for an acceleration of both drivers, to include access to higher education among the basic entitlements enjoyed by citizens in democratic societies; and to "put knowledge to work" in order to generate wealth and to improve the quality of life. The prospects for higher education during the same period are also relatively easy to predict increased efficiency (which is likely to include growing pressure to make students contribute more to the cost of their higher education); greater accountability, although more probably in a "market" than a "planning" mode as even the state redefines its role as the purchaser of higher education services, more differentiation, both between and within higher education institutions, as they struggle to identify markets niches; and possibly growing demands that higher education become more relevant as instrumental considerations triumph over idealistic ones.

However, the future may be more complex than the past. In the second half of the 20th century the encounter between higher education and society has been comparatively straightforward. Although dynamic, society has presented a familiar enough face. It was characterized by a combination of bureaucratic rationality and secular (and liberal) individualism. The beneficence of science and technology was uncontested. The dominant economic model was of large scale industry, or analogous organisations in the corporate and public sectors. Although rapidly evolving, concepts and categories like "career" and "profession" remained valid. Higher education too was familiar enough. Despite the great expansion of student numbers and its adoption of novel roles, the university continued to be recognizable as such. Other types of higher education institution have been deeply influenced by university values and practices.

In the first half of the 21st century both society and higher education may become problematical and so contested categories. Some of these uncertainties are already emerging. Once firm demarcations between public and private domains, whether in terms of the balance between the state and the market or between social "spaces" and individual desires; between producers and users; between investment and consumption; between work and leisure are becoming increasingly fuzzsy in the emerging post-industrials society. Wealth is being generated by the production of "symbolic" as well as—or more than—material goods. Value is created by design, sales, marketing, service rather than by primary production. Institutions of all kinds, civic and corporate, are being challenged by the rise of adaptable and flexible organisations, made possible by advances in communications and information technology.

The force of globalisation amounts to much more than round-the clock-round—the world financial markets or an emerging international division of labour; it is not only undermining nation states but also reconfiguring time and space to produce global intimacies, again with the help of the information revolution. Social identities are no longer moulded by the "givens" of religion, class and gender, or by positions within the occupational structure, as they have been since the advent of the industrial revolution in Europe two centuries ago. Instead they are being subsumed by a process of individualisation in which life-styles rather than life-chances predominant.

Higher education will have not only to continue to satisfy the predictable demands for democratic entitlement and socio-economic utility with which it is familiar, but also to cope with the consequences of these new uncertainties. These may include; new curricula that emphasis style and images at the expense of skills and information; recategorisation of higher education as a playful, even selfish, activity; a tighter link between experience of higher education and social esteem; submergence of the universal, but also particular, values characteristic of the traditional university by anomic globalisation; threats to the scientific tradition and methods, from the "risk society", from subjectivisation and from demands that other knowledge traditions are accorded equal respect.

The universities of the 21st century, therefore, may

have to face two ways. They will have to continue to pay attention to the democratisation and the "knowledge society" agendas, which are likely both to be subsumed in a larger "lifelong learning" agenda. Their ability to sustain current levels of public funding and to satisfy their student-customers will depend on their success in this respect. It will not be easy. There is a danger that the essence of higher education will be lost if it succumbs to unconstrained populism. If this happens, the "quality" of the university will disappear- and with it perhaps its distinctiveness and so its utility and marketability. Similarly in the knowledge Society of the future the university will face new rivals because all organisations will need to become "learning organisations". These rivals strength will be increased if the superiority of universal science is successfully challenged.

But universities will also have to address the new agendas or the "death" of work (land graduate careers?), of new social movements (and the erosion of individual enlightenment, of globalisation and virtualisation (and the undermining of academic community?); of "alternative" knowledge traditions and, perhaps even, anti-cognitive values with the undermining of "objective" science and further erosion of a common intellectual culture.

15

Solving the Unemployment Problem by Looking Beyond the Job

If you had a job, you worked; if you didn't, you didn't. Having a job meant being employed by an organisation in a clearly-defined and stable occupational role, with duties, hours, rates of pay and promotion all more or less standardised. But the job—in that meaning of the world—is a social invention, and a fairly recent one.

The job—the kind that you had, or hoped to get—because a central fixture of life. Its importance was great because it served many needs: For managers and efficiency experts, job assignments were the key to assembly-line manufacturing. For union organizers, jobs protected the rights of workers. For political reformers, standardised civil service positions were the essence of good government. Jobs provided an identity the immigrants and recently-urbanised farm workers. They provided a sense of security for individuals and an organising principle for society.

Jobs functioned in so many ways that it is surprising how many organisations are now opting for other ways to define and manage work. The second job shift is underway. Its emergence can be seen in the increasing use of temporary and part-time workers and contracted-out services, the changing relationships between workers and management, the growing popularity of self-employment and small business. Indeed, "de-jobbing" is proceeding at such a pace that many economists, management experts and futurists are now taking freely about the end of the job. Bridges predicts that the job as we now know it will disappear entirely—replaced by new kinds of flexible work assignments in post-job organisations—and be remembered only as a quaint artifact of the industrial age.

One reason for the change in work is the economic rules of the survival game among organisations that employ workers. To stay successful in today's hi-tech consumer economy, business have had to re-model themselves into what some experts call "agile companies"—ones that are able to respond quickly to conditions in ever-changing, fragmenting, competitive markets.

The "knowledge worker", whose work involves not simply doing something, but also applying theoretical or analytical skills. Such workers are replacing the industrial labourer as the dominant part of the workforce—and their productive activities are likely to be organised and structured much differently from those of their assembly-line predecessors.

De-jobbing as a result of new technology or the emergence of a service economy is a phenomenon that gets a lot of attention these days; but it is not the whole story. At all levels of society, people are improvising livelihoods that do not fit the industrial-era model. Immigrants to the developed countries, often unable to find steady jobs, nevertheless find places in the new landscape by being mobile, flexible, resourceful and imaginative: they moonlight, work part-time, share jobs, start small businesses. Their lives are often extremely difficult, but they are also instructive to those of us who believe you either have a job or you're out of luck.

It is too early to evaluate the implications of this multifaceted transformation of work, or to dismiss it as simply good or bad. Nevertheless, one cannot deny that it is taking place, and will bring about dramatic social changes.

On the downside, the job shift is causing great hardships for many workers and their families. It poses serious challenges to policy-makers, political activists and labour leaders. The basic question appears to be whether the key to global employment-development strategy is to play "catch-up"—trying to bring millions of people around the world into jobs in industries and the public sector, or to play "leapfrog"—creating new forms of employment.

The proposal to generate more employment in agriculture, for example, is based on new demand for agricultural exports from developing countries. The policies designed to make the most of this opportunity include measures to upgrade technology, raise productivity, ensure the supply of essential inputs, establish marketing and distribution channels, create links between agriculture and industry, and cater to export markets.

The issue of part-time work, another kind of employment that is seriously undervalued in the traditional industrial era job mind-set. Part-time work may not offer much at this point to developing countries, where many people are under employed and wages are low, but it can be of great help in more advanced economies. And it is likely to be a big part of the global work picture in the years ahead.

A certain agility may also be necessary in agriculture, particularly in countries that for many years have depended heavily on producing commodities such as sugar for export as a means of generating income and employment. As Northern laboratories develop non-agricultural substitutes for many of these commodities—and this is already beginning to happen—the bottom may fall out of "monoculture" economies, only economic, but will have long-run political implications as communities attempt to reorganize themselves in response to the changed conditions. It is, therefore, in the interest of raw materials exporters to closely monitor current trends in biotechnology and the use of genetic resources and modify their internal policies in anticipation of potential long-term effects.

This calls for flexibility, and an ability to get information and to act on it. Government officials, development workers, community leaders and individuals will, in some respects, all have to be "knowledge workers" if they are to keep ahead of global changes. Jobs are going to be created not just by putting people to work, but by finding—or creating—new niches where they can be productive.

It is still possible to talk about jobs for all, and to resist the assumption made by many economists that high levels of unemployment are now inevitable. But, as we move ahead into the global information economy, we may be moving back into an older conception of the job, and seeing it again as something you do, rather than as something you have—or that has you.

16

Population Growth and Jobs

Since mid-century, the world's labour force has more than doubled, from 1.2 billion people to 2.7 billion, outstripping the growth in job creation. As a result, the United Nations International Labour Organisation estimates that nearly 1 billion people, approximately 30 per cent of the global work force, are unemployed or underemployed (working but not earning enough to meet basic needs). Over the next half-century, the world will need to create more than 1.9 billion jobs—all of them in the developing world—just to maintain current levels of employment.

As economists often note, while population growth may boost labour demand (through economic activity and demand for goods), it will most definitely boost labour supply. During the next 50 years, almost 40 million people will enter the global labour force—defined as those between the ages of 15 and 65 seeking work—each year. Between 1995 and 2050, some 1.9 billion additional jobs will need to be created to absorb these new would-be workers. The most pressing needs will be found in the world's poorest nations—a sobering example of the vicious cycle linking poverty and population growth.

As the children of today represent the workers of tomorrow, the interaction between population growth and jobs is most acute in nations with young populations. Nations such as Peru, Mexico, Indonesia, and Zambia with more than half their population below the age of 25 will feel the burden of this labour flood. In the Middle East and Africa, 40 per cent of the population is under the age of 15. Since new entrants into the labour force were born at least 15 years ago, measures to reduce population growth have a delayed effect on the growth of the labour force, highlighting the urgency of taking action on population.

Nowhere is the employment challenge greater than in Africa, where at least 40 per cent of the population lives in absolute poverty. Although 8 million people entered the sub-Saharan work force in 1997, by 2030 this resource-scarce region will have to absorb more than 17 million new entrants each year. Over the next half-century, Nigeria's labour force is projected to grow by 246 per cent and Ethiopia's will soar by 337 per cent—both faster than growth of the general population. At current growth rates, the size of the labour force in sub-Saharan Africa will more than triple by 2050.

As a result of unprecedented population growth and increasing acceptance of female participation in the work force, the number of people seeking jobs in the Middle East and North Africa, a region already plagued by double-digit unemployment rates, will double in the next 50 years. In Algeria, where unemployment stands at 22 per cent, the labour force is growing at a staggering 4.2 per cent annually, and the number seeking work will more than double by 2050. Egypt alone will need to create 26 million more jobs by 2050 as its total population hits 115 million.

Nations throughout Asia will also see phenomenal increases in the numbers seeking work, including Pakistan, where the work force will grow from 70 million in 1998 to 205 million by 2050. Over the next 25 years, India will add nearly 10 million to its work force each year. During the same period, China will add nearly 6 million annually due to population growth alone, compounding the work shortages caused by the current flood of migrants to China's coastal cities and by massive layoffs—estimated at more than 30 million—as state-run operations are scaled back.

Nations are hard-pressed to educate and train rapidly growing numbers of young people in marketable skills for the global workplace. Moreover, meeting the basic needs of a growing population draws scarce foreign exchange and other resources from investments in education and job creation. Throughout the world, young people entering the work force are increasingly faced with unemployment and social marginalisation. In most societies, unemployment rates for those under 25 are substantially higher than for older people.

Surplus farmland once served as a traditional source of employment for growing populations, as new land could be ploughed to generate work and income. However, global percapita Greenland has dropped by half and considerably more in certain nations since 1950. Moreover, the mechanisation of agriculture fuels the exodus of job seekers into the world's urban areas, where unemployment is often most acute, heavily reliant on natural capital in the past, future job creation will require massive amounts of financial capital to jump-start the industrial and service sectors.

As the balance between the demand and supply of labour is tipped by population growth, wages—the price of labour—tend to decrease. And in a situation of labour surplus, the quality of jobs may not improve as fast for workers will settle for longer hours, fewer benefits and less control over work activities.

Employment is the key to obtaining food, housing, health services, and education, in addition to providing self-respect and self-fulfilment. Rising numbers of unemployed people could drive global poverty and hunger to precarious levels, fueling political instability.

17

Beyond Economics

Unless policymakers take a more all-round view of education, they risk sending their countries down the wrong path. Over the past decade, educational change in most countries has been driven by one imperative: survival in the global economy. This process has been particularly salient in the Asia-Pacific region following the drastic shock of the 1997 economic downturn. But in the current reform process, marked by speeding commercialisation and economic preoccupations, other educational missions are being ignored, and countries risk paying a high price for their short-sightedness.

There's no denying that economic considerations are critical in today's world. Students have to acquire the knowledge and skills to survive and compete in the global economy, especially one which more than ever before prizes human capital. A high-quality labour force gives nations a cutting edge in global competition. Understandably, stressing economic returns in the current educational debate attracts private resources. But education has other functions that are the indispensable corollary of more balanced, equitable development. They deserve to be briefly explained.

The first is a social function: education has a role to play in facilitating social mobility and bringing about integration in often very diverse constituencies. It is at school that children learn how to form a broader set of relationships, to live together and become aware of belonging to teach us civic attitudes, to make us aware of our rights and responsibilities—in essence, to become responsible citizens. The task is fundamental in light of democracy's advance in so many countries over the past decade or so. Then there is education's cultural function. Developing creativity and aesthetic awareness, accepting other traditions and belief systems while valuing our own are all part of the path towards fulfilment. Finally, education is a goal in and of itself. Schools help children learn how to learn and play a pivotal role in transferring knowledge from one generation to the next. I believe that all these facets of learning are critical for the long-term prosperity of our societies. In our globalised, interdependent world, these functions take on a more international character. Everywhere, education has a role to play in eliminating racial and gender biases, promoting global common interests, moments for peace, and greater international understanding.

Rising Above Short-term Pressures to Strike a Harmonious Balance

While education is widely recognised as the spine of the learning society, the complexity lies in striking a balance between these various functions. The commercialisation of education that we are witnessing the world over inevitably pushes schools, educators, parents and policymakers to pursue short-term, market-driven outcomes. Lawyers, bankers and businessmen have an increasingly high profile in educational debates. Following Southeast Asia's downturn in 1997, they were influential in changing the academic mindset. In little time, emphasis has shifted from academic achievement to developing communication skills, creativity, adaptability. In and of itself this is not necessarily regrettable. The problem is that these skills are all perceived to be at the service of a supreme economic value.

Sounder research will be required to analyse and assess where the current trends are leading us. It is increasingly recognised, however, that unless economic growth is accompanied by good governance, a fair sharing of benefits, better social and environmental protection and attention to culture, it will, sooner or later, lead to unrest. It is through education that this broad spectrum of concerns can be nurtured. Policymakers who have taken stock of this holistic mission unfortunately represent a minority in today's educational debates and reforms. Their foremost challenge is to manage commercialisation, to rise above short-term pressures and to take a more ethical stance towards education, a long-term strategic view.

18

Violence in School

A World Wide Affair

In all countries, schools are magnets for strife in society, dealing with these tensions calls for extreme caution, for fear of making matters worse. Violence in schools is a world wide problem: it exists in rich and poor countries alike. It's chiefly a male phenomenon, hitting a peak when boys turn 16 years old in some countries and 13 in others. Experts agree at least on one point: this violence cannot be pinned to a single cause. Instead, they point to complex patterns linked to family situations. Socio-economic conditions and teaching methods.

Tackling Segregation

But these are just indicators and do not justify any deterministic explanations. When researchers say that 10 to 20 per cent of risk factors are linked to single parent families, this suggests that 80 to 90 per cent of such families are not the source of any violence. A child from a slum area with a teenage mother or a father in jail will not automatically be violent! Likewise, experts say there is a "hard core" of violent children—about five per cent of the total. One can found that this figure can vary between one and 11 per cent. The school itself can be an aggravating factor, though high staff turnover or "ghetto classes" to which poorly-performing students are relegated. These "hard core" groups, then cannot be deemed "inalterable". On the contrary, something can be done about them.

Should they simply be expelled, as some advocate? Such a measure would only make their segregation and sense of exclusion worse. And they are, after all, at the root of the whole problem. The solution lies partly in developing customized projects, but most importantly, in strengthening economic social participation.

To put an end to school violence, we need a well-established state with the means to compensate for inequalities, a state that tries to re-establish diversity in neighbourhoods and schools, one that does not give up on the notion of justice for children, as some are demanding.

Passing the Torch

We should also try to life schools out of their fortresses, so they do not become the symbol of a society that excludes people. Projects in the Netherlands, Brazil and the and the United States have shown that schools can be vibrant places that provide social, medical and cultural services to a neighbourhood.

In the Brazilian state of Minas Gerais, for example, there is a vocational school where elderly craftsmen teach their skills to teenagers. Such contact between generations can offer a very valuable social education. "It takes a village to educate a child", goes an effort an African proverb. Let's make an effort to seek out these opportunities, even in the most heartless cities.

19

Rural Poverty in India

"It is morning in a remote farming area in India. As her husband harnesses a bullock to plough their field, a women pounds the grain she will use for the day's main meal. Three kilometres away, their children are collecting fuel wood and water before starting their morning walk to school".

"After School, they help their mother light a fire with a few sticks, milk the cow and collect the sundired grain. That evening, as the family rests around the hearth, father worries about how to sell his onions before they spoil and the price falls. Before sleeping his wife prepares a basket of home-grown vegetables to sell next day at the village market five kilometres away. With the takings, she hopes to buy a kerosene lamp although she might not have enough cash left to buy the kerosene immediately...."

That description of rural life is a daily reality for hundreds of millions of families throughout India. Rural poverty, 1990s means subsistence on the meagre earnings of wage labour or unreliable harvests from small plots of land. It means raising a family without safe drinking water or proper sanitation, suffering disease or injury without medical assistance. In times of unemployment or crop failure, it means living with the pangs of hunger—and the risk of death by famine.

Inside the Poverty Trap

Poverty in rural India is created and perpetuated by a number of closely interlinked socio-economic processes.

1. Policies and institutional arrangements biased against the poor exclude them from the benefits of development, frustrate their productive potential and accentuate the impact of other poverty processes.

   Institutional processes that perpetuate rural poverty include lack of access to land, inequitable share-cropping and tenancy arrangements, poor markets, limited access to credit, inputs and technology, and ineffective extension services. Other constraints are lack of training facilities, inadequate research related to small-holder farming system, and last but not least a lack of grass-roots institutions needed to foster people's participation.

   Policy and institutional biases have short and long-term impacts. In the short term, the poor are unable to earn enough to meet nutritional requirements or to take advantage of the market. "In the longer term", "poor households continue to lag behind because they do not generate a surplus for investment, nor do they have access to investment opportunities. Moreover, the rural poor may be forced to overuse resources, which undermines productivity and income".

2. Even today dualistic agrarian structures originating in colonial times persist. In Indian, highly capitalized large and medium-sized farms have virtually monopolistic control over land and labour at the expense of the small farm sector. Large scale commercial producers— control the best farm land. Resources have been funnelled into irrigated plantations producing cotton and mechanized cultivation of sorghum. In marginal areas, mechanisation has led to environmental degradation and the loss of seasonal grazing and stock routes for pastoralists.

"Thus, side by side with modern agriculture, millions of marginal farmers and herdsmen far below the poverty line". This dualism severely limits their capacity to grow food and accumulate capital. They lack marketable surpluses, and incentives and opportunities to save and invest.

3. Rapid population growth can cause and perpetuate rural poverty by increasing pressure on limited productive resources, social services and employment, as well as paradoxically—creating labour shortage through outmigration.

   The most obvious consequence of rapid population growth is that, even with relatively high rates of economic growth, improvements in living conditions are limited. Total saving in the economy declines, leaving fewer resources for investment in human development. Negative consequences are most acute in rural areas. Growing population often combined with traditional laws of inheritance—has led to fragmentation of holdings, degradation of crop and pasture land, and falling yields. In areas with unequal distribution of land, rapid population growth has accelerated proletarisation of the rural work force and reduced incomes.

4. Rural poverty malnutrition and undernutrition are closely linked to environmental degradation. Poor people in marginal areas are destroying natural resources as they struggle to keep their production systems sustainable. In acute shortage of arable land has forced farmers to reduce the length of fallow periods and plough up land previously reserved for grazing. These practices have led to declining yields, soil depletion and further impoverishment. Population pressure is pushing weaker members of the rural community into ecologically vulnerable areas.

   Degradation of the environment is strongly linked to household food insecurity and lack of fuel. Much of the fragile forest cover has been destroyed by poor rural people in the search for grazing land and fuel wood.

   Government policies have also wrought environmental damage. A rapid expansion of areas under crops often accelerates deforestation and land degradation.

Programmes to expand cereal production into marginal areas, subsidized capital to support commercial operations subsidies for inappropriate technologies and excessive transfer of income out of the agricultural sector may undermine the sustainability of smallholers and pastoralists' production systems.

Inadequate public investment in off-farm employment and infrastructure, a lack of price incentives and inadequate access to modern agricultural inputs and services discourage investment in land conservation, leading to further overuse and degradation.

5. As poverty undermines traditional social bond, the marginalisation of women has become a fact of rural life in India. With little or no access to land, million of women depend on casual employment on meagre wages. Often, they farm fragmented plots of poor quality. Limited access to inputs, extension, training and credit limits, in turn, their ability to enter commercial agriculture.

The exodus of males in search of work in urban areas (itself an indicator of poverty) has serious consequences for the women they leave behind. Output from land often falls and less attention is paid to maintenance, setting the stage for a long-term decline in productivity. Many female headed households have abandoned the use of oxen for ploughing, some plough and plant late and other no longer weed their fields.

6. The ethnic or cultural marginalisation of tribal or minority populations also plays a role in poverty. Many of these groups are further threatened by newly marginalized groups as the expansion of cultivation reduces and grazing areas of nomadic herders.

7. Exploitative middlemen also perpetuate rural poverty. Landlords exploit share croppers and tenants, moneylenders exploit debtors, and traders exploit small scale producers. During seasonal food shortages, the poor may have to borrow money at interests rates exceeding 20 per cent a month. Forced to devote most

of their energies to debt servicing, they sink deeper into the poverty trap.

In some cases, government controlled co-operatives and government agencies whose task is to protect the poor may themselves practise forms of exploitation. Heavy levies imposed by government agencies have damaged small farmers. Large, inefficient bureaucracies are paid for by the productive sectors of the community and frequently contribute to accumulation of large budget deficits.

8. Political troubles and civil strife have had a disastrous impact on the rural poor one effect is the disruption of development assistance to the rural poor, both from national and international agencies. Another is the transformation of many producers into consumers of social services with serious consequences for production, savings, capital accumulation and investment.

9. The international economic environment directly influences the well-being of the Indian poor. Falling commodity prices and protectionist policies in India affect the employment and incomes of plantation workers and small-holders producing for export, particularly those relying heavily on a few agricultural commodities. Changes in international interest rates have repeatedly hurt small-scale producers in debt-burdened India, while world grain price increases has triggered rural famines.

The net flow of development resources to agriculture also affects rural poverty. Official development funding for food and agriculture increased between 1975 and 1982, but has fluctuated irregularly since. Moreover, concern with trade balance is diverting resources to export crops, sometimes at the expense of traditional crops grown by poor farmers.

20

Employment and Poverty Alleviation

Today the key socio-economic problem is large-scale unemployment. Spreading joblessness brings many other problems in its wake. It erodes national income and living standards, aggravating the already grindingly difficult job of promoting development and alleviating poverty. Joblessness also raises government budget deficits, increasing macro-economic instability while soaking up investment for productive capital expenditure, education, training and relief aid. And joblessness ruins lives and communities by depriving people of the dignity and satisfaction that comes with earning one's keep and making a contribution to the well being of family and society.

Theories about how best to nurture development (and thus create jobs) have shifted considerably over the last decade. The state role has evolved, in the minds of many, from being a source of relief for the problems of unemployment, poverty and underdevelopment, to being a fundamental cause of these problems through the distorting impact of its intervention on the market.

However, the more market oriented philosophy that grew up during the 1990s has yet to provide convincing solutions in practice at least not on a grand scale and especially not in terms of job creation as the present jobless economic recovery demonstrates.

The weakness of the current recovery and past approaches to economic development can be traced to the failure to consider employment as the predominant means of promoting growth and alleviating poverty. In policy circles it has too long been an almost ignored priority.

Current trends thus bode poorly, particularly as unemployment rates soar. In light of the circumstances, we need to begin re-examining some of the fundamental questions—if only to find out what has gone wrong with the answers.

Minimum Wage?

Let's begin with wages. With corporate restructuring in full force on a global scale, are low wage rates required to raise employment and maximize profits? A top manager of a multinational consumer electronics group certainly thinks so; he likened the perfect factory to a ship "so that we could move it around the world to where labour was cheapest". Perhaps, but this bottom-line emphasis on unit labour costs ignores at least two other factors; namely, that higher wages can act as a screen to select more productive workers and that higher wages translate into better productivity via improved worker nutrition, increased consumption and a generally healthier quality of life.

If higher wages bring these benefits (and it is an open question) should government insist that there be a minimum wage rate? Neo-classical economists tend to respond "no", assuming that a higher wage rate puts money into the pockets of some low wage workers while forcing many others out of work because companies cannot afford to pay them.

Technology Transfer

The impact of technology is another area in need of study. Technological innovation is usually labour-saving and tends to originate in industrialised countries, moving toward developing countries like India, Pakistan where labour tends to be low cost and abundant. Would it therefore make sense to slow down or somehow restrict technology transfer, especially to development markets, in the interest of preserving employment?

The answer here is clearly—no. Historical evidence abundantly demonstrates that attempts to retard technological progress bring about grater poverty and lower growth. Technology, infact, is at the heart of the new endogenous growth theory which is very much in vogue among development economists today. Slowing down or inhibiting technology transfer would certainly dash many countries' development hopes and aggravate poverty. However, the relationship between technology, development, employment and poverty alleviation is not without its complications.

In the 1980s, the buzz word among development specialists was "appropriate technology", i.e., small-scale and labour-intensive technologies that would increase productive output while allowing an equilibrium solution to be found such that the ratio of the productivity of labour to that of capital is proportional to their relative prices. The conditions for this "small is beautiful" approach to technology tended to be best met in agricultural production. However, where manufacturing industry is concerned, the small-is-beautiful approach foundered badly when the only viable technological alternatives proved to be highly capital-intensive.

Development Gap

A wide gap has emerged between developing countries with an inward focus (which tended to be projectionist and pursue policies of import substitution) and those with an outward focus and a policy of pursuing export-led growth. Competing in international markets requires technology that is as good as or better than that found in advanced, industrialised nations. Small, therefore, is not beautiful in the global manufacturing economy where product standards are high and the elasticity of substitution between labour and capital is very limited.

The drive to obtain state-of-the-art technology thus leads to a policy conundrum: it is a pre-condition for success in manufactured exports, but the impulse to compete successfully in this most lucrative sector speeds up the transfer of technology from the developed to the developing world, thus reinforcing the bias toward labour saving equipment in developing countries and accelerating a process that is seen as a source of job loss in the industrialised countries.

Technology and Jobs

Before concluding that modern technology transfer is inimical to employment in developing countries, we have to distinguish clearly between technology's static and dynamic consequences. In a static sense, it is true that highly capital-intensive export industries may not create much employment on a net basis, but the dynamic effects of technology transfer do contribute to economic growth. And growth, in turn, generates multiplier effects in the form of demand, which stimulates ancillary production activities (like food processing or consumer goods) that rely on more labour-intensive technologies.

The problem is that the diffusion and application of technology on a global scale blurs the categories of international product specialisation and creates a much more competitive and conflict-prone international environment.

For example, we have already seen the Asian Tigers move from producing goods such as textiles and processed food to producing hi-tech and value-added consumer durables. This advance is only possible due to the growth of human capital (facilitated by investment and higher incomes) and it leaves production of textiles to other industrializing countries, like Indonesia, the Philippines and now China. But the dynamic comes at the expense of jobs in industrialised regions, like the US and the EC, which lost more than a quarter of their work force in textiles during the 1980s. Inspite of job losses, advanced countries continue to produce textiles, notwithstanding major differences in the hourly wage rates for spinning and weaving and the fact that essentially the same hi-tech equipment is being used in most production centres.

Protectionism

What has happened in textiles is happening in other industrial sectors (automobiles, for example) as well. The intense market competition is providing to be a source of trade conflicts, and possibly protectionism, as jobs come under increasing pressure.

For many workers and managers, the benefits of foreign direct investment look increasingly like a zero-sum game for employment, and there is a real risk that the tenuous link between overall growth and employment will break down altogether. It is hardly surprising that we are already seeing negatively affected workers and local businesses clamouring for protection in advanced countries.

Governments Role

The concerned governments are suppose to carry out much of this research. The three initial lines of inquiry follow from three reasonable assumptions about the future.

- First, increase in welfare and consumption subsidies are out; investments in training and human capital are in. How can investments in human capital be directed to positive employment effects? Is it perhaps not time to explore more fully benefit schemes targeting the unemployed and the unskilled poor providing them with the type of subsidies that would enhance their human capital, improve their health and productivity through better nutrition and preventive medicine, and restore the dignity of holding a job?
- Second, given the quasi-inevitability of increased automation in manufacturing, how can other sectors (particularly agriculture and services) be developed to export their long-term potential for employment creation?
- Third, given the inevitable pressures of work and productivity in the global economy, what sort of alternative institutional arrangements need to evolve

with respect to industrial relations, employment and work conditions?

Finding answers to these and other questions will require no small amount of new thinking, but parochialism or a failure of imagination would be fatal flaws in this global era.

21

Women and Poverty

It is becoming more evident that the majority of the poor in developed and developing worlds are women. Poverty among rural women is growing faster than among rural men. Over the past 20 years, for example, the number of women in absolute poverty rose by 50 per cent as against some 30 per cent for rural men. The alarming evidence concerning the underlying trends for this process strongly indicates that the gender composition of the poor is veering towards a greater share of women.

Poverty manifests itself in many ways among migrant and refugee women, elderly women and children and indigenous women. Poverty is a complex, diverse and dynamic condition stemming out of depravation with respect to income, from social inferiority, isolation, physical weakness, powerlessness and humiliation.

Analysis of women's poverty suggest that its main causes stem from the perpetual disadvantage of women in terms of their position in the labour market, access to productive resources and income for the satisfaction of their basic needs. They also demonstrate that poor women possess exceptional resourcefulness, initiative and entrepreneurial spirit and that they show tenacity and self-sacrifice in trying to take a long-term view of their poor economic conditions and in safeguarding their livelihoods.

Development is the most important challenge facing the human race. The lack of progress in the last twenty years in the eradication of poverty and growing proportion of women among the poor is the single most important threat to the progress of development and its sustainability. As long as three-quarters of the world population continue to suffer from acute depravation, as long as profound imbalances in global consumption continue to persist, and, more important, as long as the spread of poverty, particularly among women, continues unchecked, there can be no development. The history of the development process shows again that the economic status of women is the key variable in the solution to the poverty crisis. It is time for the full recognition of the fact that women are part of the solution to poverty and to the stagnating development, not part of the problem.

The Earth Summit in Rio, the Human Rights Conference in Vienna, the Population Conference in Cairo and the Beijing Conference all were milestone events in terms of advancing our understanding of the crucial role of women in development and focusing the attention of the international community on the issues concerning the role of women in the work place and in society. All of them drew attention to women's full and effective participation in development. None, however, full articulated how to achieve this challenging task.

It is important to retain focus on the issue of economic potential when discussing poverty among women because it is clear that power is only meaning something in practical terms if it is reinforced by economic power. Women have the means to transform productive resources into such power if only enabling environment is created. It is not the lack of capabilities, but that of resources, which is clearly responsible for women's poverty.

Sometimes the so badly needed resources are not even truly scarce. Billions have been wasted on arms purchases around the globe and particularly in the countries, which can not afford such misallocation of public funds. At the same time, women's organisations from grassroots to the international level are poorly funded. Such misallocation of resources at the time when poverty among women is increasing, is immoral and unacceptable, not only on the part of the governments which pursue such wasteful policies, but also on the part of the suppliers, who in most cases are developed economies.

Government's responsibilities do not end here. It is extremely important, and indeed it is the main duty of every government around the world, to provide a conducive environment for economic growth and stability by pursuing responsible and sound macro-economic policies, which will enable the economy to grow without marginalizing women. When inflation is rampant, when political climate is unstable, leading to conflicts and civil strife, little can be done for poverty alleviation.

22

Towards a New Policy on Poverty Reduction

In recent years, the call for the policy which enables the reduction of mass poverty in India has increased not only from scientific point of view, but also from political and practical standpoint. Mass poverty is a problem crucial not only for the people concerned, but also for the future of humanity as a whole, and one that cries out for rapid solution. Indians still have not succeeded in permanently improving the living conditions of big parts of their population. Measures in terms of economic growth expected by Indians over the past fifty years, the preliminary growth-oriented development strategies pursued hitherto have not been unsuccessful. Many poor population groups continue to be excluded from the economic growth. The "Trickle-down effect" has failed still fails to reach them.

Marginalisation

As a result, the course development took in India led to the marginalisation of broad sections of the population. Marginal groups arose that were denied access to the development process. They are characterized by a lack of active participation (exclusion from decision-making processes) and passive participation (failure to receive goods, services and social services). Such groups found themselves in a vicious circle. Because of their marginality they achieved only low rates of labour productivity and remained poor. They consequently slipped further towards the fringe of development. The greater the progress attained by the other sectors of the economy, the more acute the marginalisation process became. The numerical increase in membership of these marginal groups was so great that in course of time they came to constitute a considerable proportion of the population.

This mass poverty is unacceptable not only from a humanitarian point of view. It also engenders problems of global dimensions. The increasing threat to the environment, a population growth stretching the capacity of the earth to its very limits, dramatic difficulties in India safeguarding food supplies, and the still unresolved debt crisis are only the tip of an iceberg that is to a large extent spawned and nurtured by mass poverty.

In view of this situation it seems paradoxical that the scientific literature related to the problem of mass poverty apparently finds it difficult to precisely define poverty, to ascertain its causes and to asses it in ethical, political, social and economic terms. The literature often states that there is neither a generally acceptable definition nor a more or less comprehensive and stringent theory of poverty. However, the lack of generally binding definitions of the concept is due not to the often cited difficulty of measuring the societal "quality" of poverty in quantitative terms. The reason is rather that both societies as a whole and individual social groups with differing values, religious convictions, ideologies and the resulting structures and functions, reach differing conclusions on where the line between "poor" and "not poor" is to be drawn. Views differ just as widely on the societal and individual salience of poverty. A generally valid concept of poverty applicable to every social context is accordingly not available.

Absolute and Relative Poverty

In discussing the problems of poverty, a distinction must be drawn between absolute and relative poverty. In the case of absolute poverty the insufficiency of resources available to an economic entity for the maintenance of physical subsistence is so drastic that the affected parties are no longer able to live in a manner "fit for human being". In the case of relative poverty an economic entity has insufficient resources in comparison to other economic entities. This relative poverty does not necessarily mean that those affected are unable to live a life fit for human beings. It means merely that, due to the distributional structures prevailing in an economy, individual economic entities suffer deprivation to an unacceptable degree.

Poverty can be defined in both its aspects as deprivation. The deprivation can refer to various economic, social and/or political areas of human life. Poverty then means that various economic, social, and/or political needs of certain social groups are not satisfied, or are only inadequately satisfied. How drastic deprivation must be in individual cases and in what areas it has to occur before one can speak of absolute or relative poverty depends both on the observer's concept of tolerance and standards and on the given frame of reference.

The attempt to formulate an objective and generally valid definition of poverty must be abandoned. Poverty is a complex and multifaceted problem. Since it can be caused by deprivation in different areas, there are in reality different poverty profiles. The poor are, in fact, by no means a homogenous group. There is a multitude of different poverty groups with different interest and needs, such as women and children, the rural and the urban poor, members of various ethnic group and religious communities. This can lead not only to conflict between different poverty groups but also to discord within the respective groups, hampering the formulation of consistent strategies for reducing poverty.

Varieties of Poverty

If mass poverty is to be lastingly eliminated, its causes must be recognized and purposively eradicated. This is the only way to go beyond cosmetic treatment of the symptoms to provide permanent solutions. Poverty cannot be attributed to a single cause. It can always be traced back to the aggregation of various factors deriving to a large extent from the social system concerned. The diverss contexts in which the production factors labour, capital and natural resources, technical knowledge, and the total environment relevant to development interact give birth to different "varieties of poverty". Successful projects and programmes for reducing poverty therefore require the fullest possible analysis of all the relevant elements and relationships of the concrete social system.

Other things being equal, the lower the percapita income of the population, the greater the extend of absolute poverty. Since this average income is in turn an indicator for the level of economic development, poverty can partially be explained in terms of the factors responsible for the economic underdevelopment of India. All strategies that contribute to improving the level of economic development can accordingly also provide an at least partial solution to the problem of poverty. In other words, a well-conceived development policy can at the same time be a functioning policy for reducing mass poverty as well.

Growth with Poverty

On the other side it has to be seen that economic growth is not automatically linked with poverty reduction. Historical examples of the last three decades clearly show that economic growth can go hand in hand with poverty increase. Even in cases where the above mentioned requirements of a development-promoting policy have been fulfilled, growth was accompanied by an increase in poverty due to a missing participation of broad segments of the population in this growth process. Or to formulate it more generally: Between growth and distributional justice—defined at least as reduction mass poverty—can be a target conflict which has to be solved by other measures than by additional growth politics. In fact, the more unequally income is distributed, the more probable material poverty becomes. The factors determining the interpersonal distribution structure of a country thus also contribute to explaining poverty.

For the mass of the poor, ownership of productive resources is usually limited to their own (mostly unskilled) labour. To a lesser extent they may also have property rights in land (e.g., in the case of very small scale farmer), and in material assets (e.g., simple implements). The level of education and training that determines human capital is, by contrast, usually so low that no marked improvements of their position can be expected. In most cases the poor of a society are also completely inadequately trained. With the exception of their labour, they thus dispose of no or of only very few productively utilizable resources. This is true for both the rural and the urban poor.

Their situation is made even more difficult by the fact that their resources can frequently not be used for farming or certain activities to be carried on despite adequate qualification, this can contribute just as much to poverty as repressive measures taken by big land-owners against small farmers, or the activities of criminal groups in poor urban areas. The utilisation of property rights can also be prevented by the complete absence of the additional resources (such as credits or jobs) required to carry on productive activities, or by their being available only on unacceptable conditions.

But even if the productively utilizable resources can actually be brought into use to produce goods and services, it is still not certain that an adequate level of income will be generated. At both the national and the international level, free entry to the market for the goods and services produced is not always attained. Since there are frequent legal, physical, and psychological barriers to entering the market. In some cases, certain groups are not permitted to sell in institutionally secured markets, or may do so only subject to severe restrictions in the national context, for example, ethnic minorities, adherents of certain religions, members of particular castes.

Without a doubt, the behaviour of individual groups and persons contributes to breeding or consolidating their own poverty. A decisive role is played by the relation between the culture-specific willingness to achieve, personal attitudes towards achievement and actual capacity for performance—always with reference to underlying components of poverty. However, the social systems concerned are likely to be of far greater significance in generating poverty. As a rule, the poor are a marginal group within a social system who do not participate in the political, social and economic decision-making and development processes. This marginality is not an isolated phenomenon. It is system-related and often the very rational reaction of the poor to discriminating framework conditions for their economic as well as non-economic behaviour. If the poor are not permanently to remain passive recipients of the alms of material aid, the marginalized population groups must integrated into the system. For this purpose, considerable structural and functional changes in the systems concerned are necessary, including a certain degree of redistribution of resources, of economic opportunities, and of political power in favour of the poor. The precondition for such changes is that the ruling elites realize that in the long run mass poverty must almost inevitably lead to revolution which in most cases generates dramatic losses also for the elites themselves.

The Poor Must Act

However, in India there is no or very little ability and willingness on the part of the socially dominant groups to carry out such changes to the system. Since for the foreseeable future the poor can expect no real support from the system that discriminates against them, the initiative for such changes—if one excludes the possibility of external intervention—must come from the poor themselves. They must learn to help themselves. Self-help is consequently a constituent element in poverty-oriented development strategies. Self-help measures of this sort should aim not only to improve the situation of the poor as such. They should also contribute to overall development by personal initiative. An awareness of making a real productive contribution to a society is an important factor in 'socio-psychological" demarginalisation. Such efforts at self-help should ideally develop within the group of the poor. Under the conditions prevailing in India, self-help must always be regarded as a group phenomenon and framed accordingly. Group successes generally provide the basis on which individuals gain greater opportunities to help themselves. If, however, the poor are unable to improve their situation by their own efforts, support for these efforts must be forthcoming. Such self-help support measures can be the object of a poverty-oriented development policy. They should most usefully not intervene at the level of the target group itself but—indirectly—at that of self-help support institutions, so as to avoid stifling burgeoning self-initiative efforts.

Every form of community self-help requires the participation of its members. Participation is thus not only a development instrument, but also a goal in itself, since it gives people a sense of self-respect and belongingness. It should thus be an essential component in any development strategy for reducing poverty. In contradiction to this demand, the poor are frequently treated more as objects than as subjects in the development process. The consequent lack of participation in the decision-making process can even be categorized as a primary cause of poverty. Indeed, as long as there is no genuine delegation of initiative, decision-making and implementation, democratisation will be no more than a slogan. If development is to be durable, it is essential to involve the marginalized groups in the planning and implementation of development programmes, and to give them a right of co-determination. This participation requires the poor to develop a critical awareness of their situation. They must stop accepting their poverty as more or less inevitable and adapting their behaviour to the situation. They must become conscious of their poverty and learn to regard it as deprivation. This critical awareness is the essential precondition for them being able to help themselves. Self-help and participation are thus inseparably interlinked.

Anti-poverty strategies directly addressing the target groups of the poor and which place no great value on self-help are doomed to failure in the long run. In the euphoric development policy conviction that help for self-help was the right way, it was, however, frequently overlooked that genuine self-help can only develop durably under certain minimum political, socio-cultural, institutional, and economic conditions. If such "margins for action" do not exist, the spontaneous development of self-help rapidly falls victim to the pressure of vested interests.

Gradual Approach Needed

What goals a poverty-oriented development policy would have to adopt, what strategies in reducing poverty ought to be developed, or what strategies can be successful in given contexts all depend on the concrete form taken by the circumstances as has been addressed here. At any rate, modesty is called for in this respect. However, ambitious it may sound to attempt to formulate a comprehensive policy for reducing poverty, in reality a gradual approach is to be recommended. In most cases it is expedient to restrict initial efforts to reducing material poverty, especially since theoretical knowledge has made most progress in this field.

It should always be kept in mind that anti-poverty strategies have political implications, since in essence they always amount to the redistribution of resources and political power, and the reorganisation of institutions. The less evident the impression of a "zero-sum game", the greater will be the chances of prevailing an evolutionary development vis a vis the dominant society. From this point of view, poverty-oriented development policy is always a strategy of limited conflict, and is thus always caught between the desired evolution and the risk of revolution deteriorating into chaos that seldom improves the lot of the "poorest of the poor".

23

Technological Entrepreneurship

The New Force for Economic Growth

Entrepreneurship has emerged as a major new force for change. The dynamic role of modern small business in economic growth has received fresh recognition worldwide. It is essential to promote entrepreneurship and to mobilize the dynamism of the private sector for accelerated national development. An unbridled private sector may not, however, ensure growth with equity. It is the prime responsibility of governments to create policy frameworks that enable business to apply technology for competitive advantage and for the well-being of the public.

The Changing Global Environment

As agents of change and progress, entrepreneurs start by identifying a market opportunity and matching this with social or technical innovations. They then proceed to mobilize the resources necessary to drive their business concept to its commercial realisation. The development of a product or service with a high-technology content—never easy anywhere, or at today's rapidly-changing global environment. It calls for restructuring the available technology and business development systems and developing the skills needed by a new breed of "techno-entrepreneurs" to transform innovations into market opportunities at home and abroad. It also requires reorienting the present processes and priorities of technical and economic cooperation among countries.

Amidst the global concerns of environmental preservation, poverty elimination and social development, the practical problems of entrepreneurship are not being properly addressed, even though entrepreneurs will create the bulk of enterprises, jobs and wealth.

A torrent of technology-based goods hits the market every week, ostensibly improving the quality of our lives while simultaneously creating complexity and dislocation. The pace of progress in information technologies, microelectronics, robotics, new materials, biomedical sciences, space science and other advanced technologies quickens, significantly changing the way we live. The growth of markets for these technologies also proceeds apace.

Further, technological change is taking place today against a background of growing intra-national and international disequilibria. While the transformation from State-centred to market-oriented development is opening up enormous opportunities and options, it has also caused severe short-term hardships. In order to survive and prosper in these changing times, India and its enterprises need enlightened government policies, good technical infrastructure and strong cultural roots.

Traditional production factors are giving way to a new paradigm characterised by new patterns of trade, investment and employment, and by informal networking life-long learning and technological entrepreneurship. The manufacturing sector in India continues to be dominated by food products, textiles, chemicals and other traditional industry, mainly in the public sector. However, change is coming, albeit slowly. State enterprises are being corporatised pending privatisation, and the share of knowledge-based and information-related activities in the marketplace is rising perceptibly. Restructuring policies now place emphasis (often purely rhetorical) on the role of the private sector. The legacy of decades of centrally-planned development is generally inimical to private enterprise. In turn, the private sector has been slow to respond to economic liberalisation in India and generally failed to generate the new employment necessary to absorb new entrants to the labour force.

The regulatory problems of an onerous tax structure and administration, poor access to finance and raw materials, over-regulation of labour and land use, pervasive bureaucracy and restricted markets have been significant barriers to entrepreneurial growth.

Towards Competitive Performance

The imperative of improved performance has serious implications for India if it is to survive, stay abreast and succeed. It calls for national efforts on systemic efficiency and productivity growth, the move from an investment-driven to an innovation-driven economy and sustained higher-order competitiveness; towards enhanced customer satisfaction at home and penetration of selected markets abroad. Concurrently, governments and business have to address such intractable problems as poverty, corruption and the degradation of the environment.

Creating New Technology-based Ventures

Starting a new business in India is a hazardous task. Problems are compounded when the venture is technology-based:

- Capital requirements are generally larger, while traditional banks are ill-equipped to process the perceived risk. Venture capital generally only becomes an option when the venture has documented the merits of its management, market and innovation.
- Knowledge-based ventures can benefit from linkages to sources of knowledge—e.g. the technical university or research lab. Such mentoring needs to be cultivated.
- Techno-entrepreneurs often have technical skills but usually lack the business management and marketing skills necessary for success. These need to be supplemented.

- In fields where technology is changing rapidly, it is often advantageous to make technology-acquisition arrangements. Sourcing such innovations, negotiating technology licensing agreements and protecting the intellectual property itself require special skills.
- Knowledge-based innovations are inherently more risky than others. The management of this unique risk requires assessment techniques and vision.
- Technology-based ventures often have social and environmental implications, which need to be managed carefully.
- Penetrating a competitive market requires good market intelligence, a good strategic plan and good luck.

Special Characteristics of "Techno-entrepreneurs"

The popular misconceptions are that techno-entrepreneurs are born, not made; that they take risks with other people's money and fail more often than they succeed. In fact, entrepreneur skills can be identified and developed. The entrepreneur is typically an innovator who formulates new solutions to existing problems, mobilizes resources and stimulates others to participate in his or her team. These aptitudes develop over time, often starting in childhood, as the person faces new challenges and learns from failure.

Entrepreneurial opportunities can be found in every industrializing country, community and family. Principal sources of entrepreneurs for knowledge-based ventures are often the university and government research laboratories, the large industrial and military establishments and professional service firms. Some motivations of the entrepreneur are the need to: be independent; create value; contribute to society; earn recognition; become rich or; quite often, simply not to be unemployed. Value-adding ventures with good growth potential can best be developed in an open market and in a culture which supports risk-taking.

The techno-entrepreneur anywhere has the challenge of moving a concept through the prototype and production phases towards creation of a product which meets market needs at a price consistent with the value created and with the ability of customers to pay.

Equally important, the market itself has to be developed and sustained. It is not enough to be first with a better mousetrap if one does not have the skills to educate and reach potential buyers and to set the market standard.

Hence one has to distinguish between innovators and inventors. The inventor is typically a creative person in a quest for knowledge or for producing new products, without determining in advance whether a real market exists for his or her inventions. On the other hand, the innovator draws on existing knowledge and the talents of others to develop or adapt a product or service at a volume and cost that can capture a significant portion of an identified market. The flexibility and creativity of a small entrepreneurial techno-venture may lead to more incremental and break-through innovations than can be generated by larger-sized firms in many sectors.

The pace and pattern of India's economic development now depend in large measure on its technical resource base. In this context, the key determinants are the skills to apply technology for enhanced competitiveness, as well as to create techbased ventures. Techno-entrepreneurs have to be supported by appropriate national structures and international linkages if they are to survive and flourish in an intensely competitive world.

24

Population Growth and Income

Global economic output, the total of all goods, and services produced, grew from $5 trillion in 1950 to $29 trillion in 1998, expanding more than twice as fast as population. This increase of nearly sixfold boosted incomes rather substantially for most of humanity. Growth of the world economy from 1990 to 1997 exceeded the growth during the 10,000 years from the beginning of agriculture until 1950.

Economic output per person climbed from just over @ 1,900 in 1950 to nearly @ 5,000 in 1997, a gain of 163 per cent. Although there is an enormous income gap between industrial and developing countries, the latter's economies are growing far more rapidly. Growth in industrial countries has slowed to scarcely 2 per cent a year during the 1990s, compared with nearly 6 per cent a year in developing nations.

The fastest-growing region in the world from 1990, to 1997 was Asia, which averaged nearly 8 per cent annually. This growth was led by China, whose economy has been increasing at nearly 10 per cent a year throughout much of this decade, making it the world's fastest-growing economy. Since 1980, China's economic output has doubled every eight years.

Incomes have risen most rapidly in developing countries where population growth has slowed the most, including, importantly, the countries of East Asia-South Korea, Taiwan, China, Thailand, Indonesia, and Malaysia, concentrating early on reducing birth rates helped to boost savings to invest in education, health care, and the infrastructure needed by a modern industrial society.

At the other end of the spectrum, African countries—largely ignoring family planning—have been overwhelmed by the sheer numbers of young people who need to be educated and employed. With population growth rates remaining at close to 3 per cent or more a year, most of any economic growth that occurred has been absorbed by the increasing population, leaving little to raise incomes.

The enormous growth during the 1990s, particularly in East Asia, is due to the huge increase in private capital flows into developing countries. Between 1990 and 1997, annual private capital flows increased from $42 billion to $256 billion, a gain of more than sixfold. This substantial amount of money dwarfs traditional flows in public funds under international aid programmes.

Although incomes in much of the developing world are rising rapidly, they are not rising for everyone. The World Bank estimates that 1.3 billion of the world's people subsist on $1 a day or less. For this one-fifth of humanity, trapped at a subhuman level of existence, there has not been any meaningful progress.

The sources of growth are changing. In earlier times, most of the growth was in agriculture. Since the advent of the Industrial Revolution, however, more and more of the growth has been concentrated in industry. Then beginning around mid-century, the services sector—insurance, banking, education—began to expand rapidly, accounting for most of the change in the industrial world. More recently, growth has been concentrated in the information sector as computerisation of the economy and telecommunications have grown at extraordianry rates.

The good news is that the global economy has been expanding at a near record pace during the 1990, the bad news is that the economy, as now structured, is outgrowing the Earth's ecosystem. The result is excessive pressures on the natural systems and resources. As noted in the first section of this paper, from 1950 to 1997 the use of lumber more than doubled. That of paper increased sixfold, the fish catch increased nearly fivefold, grain consumption nearly tripled, fossil fuel burning nearly quadrupled, and air and water pollutants multiplied severalfold. The unfortunate reality is that the economy continues to expand, but the ecosystem on which it depends does not, creating an increasingly stressed relationship.

If the economy were to expand only enough to cover population growth until 2050, it would need to grow from the $29 trillion of 1997 to $47 trillion. This, of course, would merely maintain current incomes, unacceptable though they are for much of humanity. If, on the other hand, the economy were to continue to expand at 3 per cent per year, global economic output would reach $138 trillion in the year 2050.

Even the first, more modest, growth projection would likely lead to a deterioration of the Earth's natural systems to the point where the economy itself would begin to decline. It is easy to foresee a scenario of continuing forest destruction, aquifer depletion, and ecosystem collapse that would lead to economic decline. If the world cannot simultaneously convert the economy to one that is environmentally sustainable—one that does not destroy its own support systems—and move to a lower population trajectory, economic decline will be hard to avoid.

25

What was Wrong with Structural Adjustment

In Defence of a Much-Maligned Strategy

After decades of stranded development theories, ideologies and paradigms, "structural adjustment", with its demands for clean fiscal policy and an end to uneconomic state enterprises, political privileges, market and exchange rate intervention and corruption, entered the aid arena like a refreshing dawn after a long night of frustrating dreams. Only the "old guard" of planned economy advocates and jealous academicians who had missed the boat were able to shut their eyes to the moral and economic justification of this liberating breakthrough in international development policy spearheaded by the Breton Woods institutions then steered by some exceptionally courageous economists.

Reaction to SAPs

As with any revolution, defeat is awaiting the pioneers at the hands of political power greed, reactionary tactics by the formerly privileged and academic envy. The principal device serving the reactionary forces as a lever of influence on the mood of the "development community" has been the identification and dramatisation of new pockets or strata of (principally urban) poverty allegedly created by structural adjustment measures, while shunning the much broader-based rise in economic activity, real incomes and sense of fair reward in the overall society, especially the rural population. That the hardship experienced by urban poor, formerly privileged under consumer price control and import subsidies to the debit depressed farm prices or maintained by grossly over-expanded public payrolls, was only laying open the camouflaged erosion of the economy and near-bankruptcy of governments and public enterprises, was conveniently downplayed.

These reactionary howls were to be expected. Not that they met the entirely innocent. There had been naively sweeping, overly assuming demands by some structural adjustment missions. But an intellectually vigorous and dynamic "development community" would have coped with the ensuing opposition, strengthened the analytical and monitoring capacities and the political will to endure also rocky roads and bitter medicines on the way to a healthier base. Instead institutional rivalry, political opportunism and emotive populism were thriving. In a way, the "development community" behaved as if it did not want its patient to become able to stand on his own feet and eventually steal its raison d'être.

Worst, the Bretton Woods institutions themselves, partly under the pressure of the emotive opposition described above fell to the temptation to rescue their lending volume, which was threatened by the frugality dictated to Third World public budgets under structural adjustment recipes, through hardship-easing loans. They thereby corrupted their creation in using it to reinforce their indispensability. As a consequence it soon turned out that some of the most obedient loan takers under structural adjustment terms experienced sharply rising indebtedness, exploited as a disqualifying symptom by the anti-structural adjustment camp.

Whatever the opinions on structural adjustment policies, the commitment to the principles of "good governance" has come to stay, at least on paper, as an almost standard conditionally for official development aid from

OECD donor countries. The realisation, matured in the implementation of structural adjustment programmes, that not the quantity of aid, but the quality of Third World governments determines the positive or negative course of development, may be regarded as the most valuable fruit of the decades-old policy debate in the 'development community". And the use of aidas a pressure or bribing factor towards "good governance" as foreign aid's least disputable purpose.

Out of the Limelight

Nothing, however, must be taken for granted. Achievement breeds its challenge! Structural adjustment, though in essence hardly disputable has been pushed out of the limelight and replaced by the oldest actor in the company: eradication of poverty, twinned with an equally perpetual endeavour at the macro-level: debt-forgiveness. This falling back to square one in donors' approach to the problems of the south, i.e., the call to alleviate poverty and priorities direct efforts to this end above all other developmental efforts—does it indicate a sell-out of constructive ideas in the "development community"? Has any noteworthy progress been achieved in the past by this approach?

By telling a frugally toiling but independent subsistence farmer that internationally his condition is classed as "poverty", deserving compassion and support by the world community and cancellation of his debts, one can hardly expect a sustainable improvement in his output, satisfaction, or self-respect and even less, when he realises that the help principally provides jobs, fringe benefits and self-importance to a gamut of intermediaries, at home and abroad.

What do those poverty advocates (the"Lords of poverty") really know about the resources, life managements, value systems and ambitions of those they generalize by the billions? The great variance in the conception of life situations, from different external viewpoints.

What the aid system can do for these rural populations classed as "poor"/"underprivileged"/"exploited", is press for justice, i.e., "good governance". The achievement of structural adjustment policy through e.g. abolishing official price and exchange rate distortions, import subsidies and exploitative state agencies, has brought massive income improvement for peasant populations, i.e. the majority of LDC inhabitants, in dimensions unreachable by whatsoever direct "attack" on rural "poverty". What people want is not being benevolently treated as poor, but being justly rewarded for their work, i.e., by access to the unmanipulated market value of their output. Slackening on structural adjustment/"good governance" conditionally under the present "10 year itch" for paradigm change means foregoing much of the potential opportunities for undoing injustice and exploitation of the masses. It should be clear where priority focus should be placed in ODA policy.

Small is Not Beautiful

The direct attack on "poverty", orchestrated by the Bretton Woods institutions under their freshly launched Poverty Reduction Strategy Paper (PRSP) campaign, is being rightly regarded as primarily an NGO domain, since most activities are expected to be carried out at local community level. This would require careful screening and coordinating of NGO activities and their integration via gradual expansion of their experience. But "small" is not "beautiful" for the development financing institution. Disbursement needs are pressing, calling for the new paradigm to quickly provide channels for another wave of loans to the "IDA Countries". Their problem of heavy indebtedness, which would principally exclude most of them from any new loan consideration, shall be solved with one stroke (which only the well-cushioned development bureaucracy can afford); debt relief against presentation of country PRSPs by the respective governments. NGOs are expected of play in the system especially the knowledge gap about the "poor" people's real wants and needs

NGOs will naturally be tempted by such expansionary boost to their involvement (referred to sarcastically as their philanthropic empire" by an African conference participant), but this will not be conducive to quality and accountability of their performance, which ideally should be based on private sponsorship in combination with strong target-group provided self-help components.

Patience and Self-Restraint

Local knowledge and initiatives cannot be obtained under time pressure. "The grass does not grow faster by being pulled". When will the "development community" learn patience and self-restraint in the approach to LDC's capacity for constructive absorption of aid programmes accompanied by a genuine sense of ownership?

After all these deliberations, how shall development policy be shaped in order to better correspond with reality, without sinking deeper into hypocrisy and frustration?

To come back to the opening question: what was wrong with "structural adjustment"? Nothing was wrong with its intent. In fact this was very right and long overdue. Its implementation, however, lacked patience, perseverance and solid support from the development community, apart from its being corrupted as a vehicle for expansionary lending policy. If aid is meant to not be an end in itself, then structural adjustment policy needs constant reinforcement, underpinned by strict lending discipline. There should be an end to irresponsible lending and easy escape from its consequences by wholesome periodic debt relief burdened on the international tax-paying community. No ODA, either loans or grants, should be made available to governments who are not in active process of implementing "good governance" principles. A monitoring unit, reporting to the donor community on government performance in regard to its "good government"? Structural adjustment commitment, should be maintained in each and receiving country by "donor consortia" comprising all locally represented bilateral and multilateral development organisations currently extending technical, financial or material assistance to the country.

In order to accommodate the poverty focus without diluting the necessary structural adjustment orientation of ODA, a division of activity-focus between the latter and the NGO sector would seem to be advantageous.

- ODA, limited to the countries abiding to structural adjustment/"good governance" conditionally, with focus concentration on sustainable physical, social and economic infrastructure principally at national and regional level, public management training, higher education and research, consultant and senior adviser services.
- The NGO sector, principally funded by private sponsorship, united to structural adjustment conditionally (but preferably grafted on local self-help initiative), with focus-concentration on the "Third World "poor", i.e. mostly at rural community and low-income township level, for amelioration of living conditions and local resource utilisation.
- Strengthening of linkages between the NGO sector and the UN Technical Agencies to mutual benefit: NGOs in need of professional information, evaluation and advice, of forum for discussion to find an actively supportive window at the agencies; the latter to maintain and develop field contact of research and policy generation, not least as a substitute for their declining project work (giving way to greater concentration on their global functions i.e., serving as information, policy initiation, and coordination/negotiation centre on topics of global concern such as e.g.: human rights, global monetary and trade systems, tropical forest and global marine resources, global and regional health threats, international standards).

In conclusion, it may be called to mind that aid and its institutions have no claim for permanence. They are justified only as temporary functions in a phasing-out process of self-help support. Any claim for unlimited continuity would breed lasting infantilisation.

26

Can Economic Growth Reduce Poverty?

New Findings on Inequality, Economic Growth and Poverty

Many people still think first of 'economic growth' in relation to poverty reduction. Indeed, their correlation is one of the most-discussed issues of combating poverty. The relationship is of great importance because if there is a clear causal dependency, reducing poverty could fundamentally be limited to measures to promote growth. However, if there was low growth or stagnation it would not be possible to reduce poverty decisively. In the opposite case, that of the phenomena having no causal relation, promising measures to reduce poverty could be taken up even without economic growth.

Hardly anyone now explicitly expresses the view that economic development trickles down automatically to the poor. Practical experience has refuted this assumption dating from the early days of development policy in the 1960s. However, a number of studies show development of growth and a decline in poverty running parallel. On the other hand, there are also examples which show that despite high economic growth, poverty is not reduced markedly. The common answer to the question this raises is thus: Yes, growth can reduce poverty, but only if additional measures oriented on the poor are taken up. This is often termed pro-poor-growth. But what that means in detail, and whether economic growth as such plays a causal role at all, is not clarified. It is worth taking a look at the arguments on the basis of more recent empirical and theoretical knowledge.

No Direct Causality Between Growth and Poverty Reduction

Among the many indicators of poverty, the income of the poor (income poverty) has the closest relationship to economic growth. An increase in gross domestic product and thus national income could, if other factors come into play be linked with an increase in the per capita income of the poor.

Such a relationship between economic growth and the income of the poor, however, cannot be described as causal, as is asserted implicitly time and again by the statement that growth is a necessary but not sufficient precondition for poverty reduction. In so far as growth and poverty reduction arise at the same time at the end of a process, they exist alongside each other. It would be almost a tautology to say that the former is the cause or part-cause of the latter. Both express the same thing, namely a change in per capita income as well, and both have similar causes. What matters is recognising what these causes are and what specific factors must come into play so that the income of the poor grows too. Growth as a "prerequisite" or "condition" is then no longer the focus; the priority is asking for specific policies that result in higher incomes for the poor. The detour in thinking about growth is not necessary. Since, however, it is based on similar factors, such as fiscal policy/ budget structure, employment policy, combating inflation, and institutional development, economic growth can also emerge if poverty is reduced. The difference of views lies in the fact that under the heading 'poverty reduction' the aim is no longer growth, but a purposeful reduction of poverty.

Therefore, in reverse, successful combating of poverty can be seen as being the cause of growth insofar as activating the capabilities of the poor and using their productive capacity of the poor and using their productive capacity triggers economic drive.

Indirect Causality Between Growth and Poverty Reduction

So even if economic growth fundamentally has no direct causal impact on poverty, growth still can reduce it indirectly. This is the case when due to positive economic development a government has greater revenue and uses the surplus for combating poverty, for example by providing such public goods as education and health services. Also in these cases, however, growth is not a compelling precondition. Even without growth greater government revenue can be achieved for example by more efficient tax collection. And leeway for social welfare spending can be gained by redistributing the budget, such as by cutting military appropriations. Furthermore, an automatic process is not given because the government can also use surplus funds for non-social purposes.

Creation of jobs due to increased economic activity can be another indirect link between economic growth and income poverty, if such a development generates income and reduces poverty. But also in this case I see no compelling causality because, for instance, industrial jobs are not necessarily open to the really poor. In addition, these positive impacts occur to a considerable extent only in the event of labour-intensive development. In many countries, however, economic growth is achieved by capital-intensive production.

Inequality, Growth and Income Poverty

If national incomes, grow, a naïve observer might assume that the income of the poor must also grow along with it. But that would be a statistical fallacy. Even if only the income of the rich grows, this results in macroeconomic statistics showing a higher per capita income. What the true conditions are is shown as soon as one divides the population statistically into income groups, such as in fifths, as is usual. It then turns out that the bald figures on average per capita growth can certainly cloak a situation where the income of the richest fifth of the population is growing fast while that of the poorest fifth is stagnating. Despite growth, the gap between the two becomes even wider.

The unequal distribution of income (and of other assets such as property and access to social services), and its connection to poverty reduction and growth has recently returned to the forefront of the debate.

It is obvious that inequality and its changes have direct effects on the poverty situation. Does inequality also have an impact on poverty via its relation to growth, because growth promotes or reduces inequality? Earlier, the predominant view was that rapid growth was linked with at least a temporary increase in inequality, so that a distinct policy of growth initially disadvantaged the poor.

The current dominant view is that growth has no foreseeable effects on inequality and that inequality changes only very slowly, in reverse, however, it is assumed that greater equality is a determinant of growth. According to that view, an indirect relationship between poverty on one side and inequality as a factor dependent upon growth on the other is not given.

That leads to the conclusion that fair distribution has more weight than growth. Fair distribution, however, does not depend upon growth. An appropriate policy is possible at any time, not only after an economic situation has improved. The notion that still shimmers through the debate that "something must be earned first before it can be distributed", is wrong. It is a matter of designing policy and the entire economic process right from the start in such a way that the surplus benefits all including the poor. Important elements of such a policy are, for example, land reform and development of finance systems.

Relationship of Growth to Poverty

According to today's conventional wisdom, income poverty expresses only a part of what poverty means. Not least through the voices of the poor themselves, it has become clear that violation of human dignity and rights, a lack of participation in decisions and exclusion from society, unequal treatment of men and women, and vulnerability are also regarded as poverty. For poverty is caused to a great degree by conflicts of power and interests. Income poverty often is not even seen as the greatest problem.

What relationship do these more far reaching characteristics of poverty have to economic growth? A direct relationship of growth to socially-related aspects such as women's inheritance rights, land rights and exclusion from decisions cannot be seen. Considerable improvements in favour of the poor can be achieved here even without economic growth.

Those who see a strong and causal connection between economic growth and poverty reduction must ask themselves what the prospects are for high growth rates and thus for a decline in poverty. Coupling poverty reduction to economic growth is problematic. If only low growth rates are to be expected.

Another question is whether continuous increases in growth are at all desirable and possible in the medium to long term. In this connection, a difference should perhaps be made between developing countries and industrialised nations. But environmental compatibility and availability of resources set limits to growth for both. Some academics assume that industrialised nations have already reached an inherent limit (stagnation theory) and that the high growth rates of earlier years will not return. Moreover, they add, full employment is no longer achievable due to, among other things, an ongoing increase in productivity, and current unemployment cannot be reduced by customary means. In any case, if growth were to be taken as the major benchmark, the prospects for a radical reduction of income poverty around the world would be modest.

Summing Up

Poverty is a complex problem and reducing it depends upon many interconnected factors that is why poverty cannot be attributed to one main cause nor its reduction based on one main strategy. Economic growth is just one strategic element among many others related to poverty reduction. An indirect causal connection between growth and poverty reduction can only be seen because governments will have a grater scope for action due to economic growth, and if they promote labour-intensive development.

Therefore growth's role in poverty reduction must be put into perspective growth cannot be the first thing that comes to mind, nor is it the golden path to reducing poverty. The simplistic theory of economic growth as the main condition obstructs the bigger picture; it clings to the underlying and ongoing belief in the trickle-down effect. Even if there is no growth or for inherent reasons there can be none, there are promising ways to take on the challenge of mass poverty in the developing countries. Up front, governments and bilateral and multilateral donors must have the political will to design economic, financial and social policies so that they are oriented on poverty in a coherent way—the result can also be economic growth.

27

Democracy and Poverty

Are they Interlinked?

Democracy assistance and poverty reduction are rightly becoming two focal—and related—issues for development assistance. Increasingly, many organisations, including intergovernmental, national and civil society, are focusing their work on these two areas. Futhermore, the relationship between these two issues is complex and ever changing. There is thus a need to develop methodologies of linking democracy assistance and poverty reduction at both the policy and programme levels. International IDEA (Institute for Democracy and Electoral Assistance) in cooperation with the World Bank and the United Nations Development Programme, is developing concrete strategies that address these two objectives in a mutually reinforcing way. Through an overall situation analysis followed by regional meetings in sub-Saharan Africa, South Asia, Latin America, the Caucasus and the Arab region, the Institute has marshalled evidence of some of the key problems that affect democracy consolidation and poverty reduction in these countries:

- Corruption and its undermining effect on popular confidence in public institutions;
- Continuing economic instability coupled with the lack of strategies for addressing the twin challenges of poverty and increasing popular participation in its alleviation;

- The extremely limited nature of citizen's influence on overall policy and decision-making processes despite the spread of formal democratic institutions;
- A trend in many post-communist states towards viewing growing poverty as a direct consequence of a transition to democracy.

In short, the evidence is not very encouraging for the prospects for democracy consolidation and poverty reduction. The critical step International IDEA, advocates is the development of an approach that not only seeks to put democracy assistance and poverty reduction on top of the development assistance agenda, but also to encourage all involved to treat them as twin elements of an integrated programme of action.

Through a focus on accountable governance, promotion and protection of citizenship and rights and increased popular participation, International IDEA believes that both democracy and poverty reduction can be addressed simultaneously. Policy recommendations are being developed and will be shared in the course of this year with governments, international organisations and civil society bodies.

International IDEA believes that democracy promotion can be used as a tool for fulfilling a variety of objectives. Democracy matters because it protects human right and preserves human dignity. But democracy also matters because it helps to address some of the most critical challenges facing states today: peace, development, economic growth and stability.

Democracy does not guarantee any one of these, but increasingly it seems to be a precondition for them in the long term. Thus, advocating democracy goes beyond being a moral issue; it becomes *fundamental* to advancing the well-being of people and the stability of states. International IDEA will continue to explore the link between democracy and the major issues facing society today—and continue to argue the case democracy.

28

Unemployment in the Poor and Rich Worlds

Different Causes, but Converging Policies?

In view of the magnitude of global unemployment, all the customary formulas offered by economists against mass unemployment—the basic socio-economic problem of modern times—appear to be quackery. Neither quantitative, nor any kin of 'qualitative', growth will be able to eliminate the disastrous worldwide lack of jobs. For ecological reasons it is impossible to include 800 million or more unemployed in the production process through corresponding growth. The resulting increase in global Gross Domestic Product would require consumption of natural resources, energy and the environment which, given even the greatest possible productivity in those sectors, could not even be sustained for two or three decades.

In addition, aiming to achieve full employment through growth will be even more difficult even in the rich economies. For it is most likely that work productivity will continue to rise worldwide. Countries such as China, which are in the initial phase of modernisation, are still producing at a relatively still low productivity rate. But that is precisely why they can achieve notable increases in productivity in a short time by importing technology from highly-developed countries. The advantage of rapid 'catch-up rationalisation', however, is being bought at the cost of rising unemployment and progressive impoverishment.

Employment through Redistribution of Work

The notion that jobs can at some time be created for 800-900 million unemployed who will work 35 or even 40 hours a week at the productivity level of the highly-developed countries of four or five decades ago is absurd. The only realistic possibility of eliminating the world's unemployment problem is by far-reaching redistribution of work and income. The change needed for that demands fundamentally new concepts of prosperity: a reflection on the philosophy of the 'life of happiness'. 'New concepts of prosperity' means that technological progress would no longer be used mainly to deliver rising per capita incomes and excessive consumption. Instead, given a sufficient material standard of living, the quality of life would be improved primarily by shortening working hours. It is about, so to speak, assigning instrumental good sense new goals. Plus reshaping socio-economic conditions in such a way that the politicians will again be compelled to orient themselves on the good of the community and humanistic values instead of filling the pockets of the wealthy. It is sheer ideology, although very persuasive, to cite 'globalisation' and its alleged 'iron laws' in defaming the welfare state, full employment and social justice as out-of-date wishful thinking. A return to the state-guided social competitive system as practised during the first decades after the Second World War is possible just as it was politically feasible to make the transition from the old order of unfettered, ruthless capitalism to the mixed economies of the social market economy types. So it is a matter of restoring the proven structures of a mixed economic system.

However, in contrast to the first postwar decades it is now not sufficient to regenerate nation-sate interventionism. Appropriate international regualtions are required. Above all, it will depend upon reversing the new laissez-faire developments in international economic relationships which today are subsumed under the buzzword 'globalisation'. That is, to oppose over-liberalisation and its disastrous social and inhuman impacts. It will depend on the broad mobilisation of the losers in the process of globalisation whether the necessary fundamental change of course can still be made in time before a catastrophe. In particular, the new myth must be opposed that declares globalisation as a kind of law of nature and thus suggests resignation and adaptation to an allegedly unavoidable process of destruction of social and human achievements.

Mass Unemployment in the Poor Economies

The employment problems in the rich and the poor hemispheres differ not only in their magnitude, but also in their causes. The wretched condition of the poor economies is due above all to historical reasons: colonialism and, in the post-colonial era, the constraints to independent development imposed by the hegemonic influence of the rich industrial states. The waste of scarce resources by international and civil wars, and the dictatorships with their upperclass luxury consumption and inefficient, thus development—obstructing exploitation structures—often supported by the industrialised nations, have for a long time repressed and in many cases destroyed autonomous development potential. The colonial and post-colonial distortion also contributed at least indirectly to the current population problems of the poor countries. The politically inflicted mass poverty and under-development stabilised or in fact brought about economic, socio-psychological and ideological mechanisms which oppose an effective population policy. As we know, the average educational level in many developing countries, especially among women, is too low to give a modern population policy a chance of success. Mass unemployment in the poor countries is the result of poverty. In this respect, it is about a production-side problem: too few resources, to little real and human capital, and the inefficient, unproductive use of much of the anyway limited added value of society. The picture is totally different in the rich countries the over-production economies.

Unemployment in Over-Production Systems

The main cause of mass unemployment in the industrialised nations has nothing to do with shortages. It is a phenomenon of surplus. Greater possibilities of production can no longer be used 'sufficiently profitably because the required demand is lacking. Production is done for profit. The necessary collateral condition is the satisfying of consumer needs. Employment is not even such a condition, but only a side effect which lapses immediately when labour-free production is technically possible. Thus, national income must be shared among wages and profits (or income from property). Profit is the difference between earnings and costs. Earnings depend upon demand. Macroeconomic costs consist mainly of wages and salaries (including social security contributions). These definitive connections mean that profit can be made only if overall demand is greater than the total cost labour. But in the final analysis this demand can only come from the profit-earners themselves. In his book, a Treatise on Money, Keynes described this nexus as the theory of the Widow's cruse. Under capitalistic conditions, labour is only sought or hired if profit can be earned with it. But as making a profit depends upon the demand for consumption and investment by the shareholders, it can be seen that the degree of employment is determined by the demand behaviour of the class that receives income from property. In this respect, the widespread belief that greater investment also leads to more employment, namely via the effect of investment in demand, is right.

Lower Wages Mean Lower Demand

The lower the level of wages, and given an unchanged total demand, the greater are the profits that can be made. But it is more likely that in the case of falling wages the overall demand will also drop. For stabilising total demand would require the recipients of income from property to increase their spending on consumption and/or investment to the degree to which wages and the consumption based on them fell.

During the last 10 to 15 years the development of profits in most industrialised nations has been very favourable. But profits would have grown more strongly if the demand of the shareholder had been much greater. This would have created more employment at the same time. Thus, it can be assumed that the profits are simply too high for the shareholders to be able to go in for meaningful consumption or make profitable investments. That is the reason for the extreme redirection of capital from fixed assets to portfolio investment. The growth of speculative (unproductive) financial transactions during the 1980s and 1990s (buzzword: casino capitalism), corresponded with a relatively weak formations of real capital.

Wage rises, of course, narrows the scope for profit. But precisely this effect stimulated efforts to improve the profit situation not only by investment in rationalisation, but also by investment in expansion aimed at the growing mass purchasing power. Since more is being invested, the profit mass also is growing according to the principle of the Widow's cruse. Too low wages, as it were, relieve the shareholders of the pressure to innovate and invest and allow them to earn their profits too easily. That is the real message of the 'purchasing power theory' of wages.

Over-accumulation and Under-consumption

Over-production has two different causes which, however, mostly occur in tandem. They are over-investment, or creation of over-capacities, on the one hand, and lack of demand due to relative saturation and an absence of mass purchasing power on the other. But the main reason for mass unemployment in the rich hemisphere currently lies on the demand side. During the first three decades after the Second World War supply and demand rose in relative balance. Economic fluctuations showed up as temporary declines in generally positive GDP growth rates. These decades of (dynamic) balance of growth are often described today as the era of 'Fordism'. Its essential feature is that rising wages ensure continuing growth of consumption, so that equally growing profits also flow relatively continuously into investments to expand capacity and create jobs. The label 'Fordism' expresses the 'simple' view of the theory for the buying power of wages which is said to have been propagated by Henry Ford I. This was that his workers should earn enough to be able to buy the cars they made.

The astonishingly balanced development of supply and demand from 1950 to the mid-1970s was due above all to postwar reconstruction and the pent-up demand of consumers who were starved by wartime economy shortages. This stimulated positive investment sentiment, and high investments brought at the same time high profits. The postwar growth that led within a short time to full employment was also linked with growth in productivity, which on multi-year average was more than twice that of the crisis period of the last 25 years. Thus, the so-called employment threshold (the GDP growth rate point at which employment growth begins) was much higher in those days than it is now, although there was full employment over a longer period. This simple fact opposes the thesis often propounded today that mass unemployment is above all related to rationalisation. It is not rationalisation per se, that is, progress that boosts productivity, which is the evil. The problem is that the mistakes in distribution policy which are rooted in capitalistic structures result in increases in supply encountering insufficient demand for goods, whereby the demand for labour drops. However, the fact that demand policy contradicts the requirements of a social ethic that is ecologically responsible and right for the interests of the poor countries was already spelled out. So if a demand-oriented growth policy is practised at all, it should be designed to be as environmentally compatible as possible. After all, there are possibilities for that, such as by expanding the production of services that spare resources. A one-hour driving lesson costs more energy than one hour of ballet instruction.

The politically initiated and implemented over-liberalisation and surrender of social prosperity to global competition since the 1970s, which reproduces the old self-destructive mechanism of laissez faire, have during the last two decades markedly accelerated the crisis development inherent in the system.

Summing Up, It is Noted that

- Full employments in the rich economies would certainly be possible by means of demand policy, but only at a high cost to the environment that is concomitant with high growth rates.
- The growth policy of the rich countries impairs the poor economies' possibilities of medium to long-term growth, since these are falling back ever further in the competition for ever scarcer and thus ever more expensive resources;
- The environmental collapse currently expected for the third or fourth generation after us, which obviously also will trigger a collapse of the world economy and—probably ahead of that—armed conflicts which today are hardly imaginable, would happen very much sooner if economic growth were to be increased to such a degree that it would bring full employment worldwide;
- In the long term, the problem of global unemployment and global poverty can only be solved by a policy of massive redistribution, and in fact a redistribution of work and income, whereby increases in productivity must be used mainly or only for shortening working hours. That is a demand, which appears to be utopian. But utopias of today often have the quality of scripting the reality of tomorrow.

29

Corruption

Where to Draw the Line?

Everyday the community is being stunned as reports of irregular practices compete for press headlines. The impression is that bribery and corruption, in one form or another is both extensive and increasing; although systematic statistics in this area are rare for obvious reasons.

What is corruption? The list of possibilities is extensive. It starts with the outright bribery of government officials and the more ambiguous question of political contributions; then there are a whole range of activities that could be considered to some degree corrupt—covering such things as the misuse of company assets for political favours, kickbacks and protection money for the police, payola to disc jockeys, sympathetic feature articles in return for advertising revenue, free revenue, free junkets for MP's and journalists, secret price-fixing agreements, obtaining parts in films for reasons not wholly related to acting ability, insider dealing of various kinds, as well as the improper use of the "old boy" network.

All these forms of behaviour have one thing in common. They are attempts to influence the outcome of a decision where the nature of that influence is not made public. Essentially the practices are nothing more or less than the abuse of power.

Reasons for Spread of Corruption

There are several reasons for this spread of corrupt practices. First the concentration of power in larger and larger units; particularly when combined with rapid growth where the channels of accountability are underdeveloped. It is also widespread in "mature" societies where highly developed networks attempt to preserve the *status-quo* and further their vested interests.

As Gunnar Myrdal, the renowned economist, succinctly put it in his classical study *Asia Drama*. "Generally speaking, the habitual practice of bribery and dishonesty tends to pave the way for an authoritarian regime, whose disclosures of corrupt practices in the preceding government and whose punitive action against offenders provide a basis for its initial acceptance by the articulate strata of the population".

While corruption inevitably undermines the political system, or organisational structure, in the long run those involved are invariably more concerned with short term. Also corrupt practices can be infectious. In certain areas companies with high ethical standards have either been forced out of business, or have had to give up their high standards, where their rivals have been willing to pay bribes to win orders.

It is sometimes claimed that "first class" companies are relatively "Clean—at least in the narrow sense—because they can afford to be. They are already powerful and influential, with a network of informal contacts and relationships, so they do not need to beg and bribe as a way of getting business. It is often the new company trying to break into a new market, or the company fighting for survival, that is the most likely to use bribes to cut corners. Hence the problem is prevalent both in periods of rapid economic growth and change, as well as in periods of economic crisis; although there is some evidence to suggest that more of it might come to the surface, usually by accident, during the latter than former.

It is also occasionally argued—usually not very convincingly—that corruption does not actually impede development but may even accelerate it by helping to by-pass bureaucratic red-tape. However, life in rarely that simple and entrepreneurs within this approach invariably ensure that all too frequently that payments are made and nothing gets done! A recipe for disaster especially as it is somewhat difficult for the aggrieved party to complain under these circumstances.

Unfair Distribution of Income

In some cases it has been know for payments to be strictly calculated as a defined percentage of the expected gain from a legislative concession. While on other occasions payments have become so institutionalised that they are virtually another form of taxation. However, the differences between a "corruption surcharge" and taxation needs to be recognised; the former are rarely made openly, they are usually unfair and rarely are they seen to be fair. In addition they usually redistribute the income in a socially regressive direction.

The important factor appears to be to ensure that, wherever possible, practices and channels of accountability are made public. In practice, there are few absolute principle, and trade-offs are inevitable. The key element is the extent to which any decision is made openly and appears to have widespread support. If deals can be kept completely private, the social and political repercussions will, at least in the short term, be minimal. But anyone working on such an assumption, who then finds his or her, activities made public, is likely to be in a dangerously exposed position.

In general, companies prefer clear and accepted codes of behaviour for everyone. But deciding on what is fair competition, as opposed to unfair advantage can be complicated and subjective as both individual and corporate standards of acceptable behaviour are conditioned by the traditions and characteristics of the society in which they operate.

What can be done to eliminate corruption in both its monetary and non-monetary forms? The first step is usually to pass a law making al teast monetary corruption an offence. It is assumed that unaccountable assets are by themselves sufficient evidence of corruption. However, there is little evidence to suggest that the extent of corruption is related to the type of legislation, as the problems of law enforcement are usually formidable in this area.

The paradox at the centre of an anti-corruption programme is that the laws must first be passed by governments and the standards set by politicians are a vital element in this process, yet these are the very people who are most likely to profit from illicit payments.

Of course, no measures against corruption are likely to be effective if officials are so badly paid that they cannot live on their salaries. As a result many have combined an anti-corruption programme with an increase in official salaries. Unfortunately, although poor pay frequently drives people to extort bribes higher pay by itself, rarely stops it. This is partly due to the perennial problem that few people consider themselves adequately paid and partly because in both the corporate and political arenas ineffective control systems provide a fertile breeding-ground for the more blatant forms of monetary corruption. In order to reduce these abuses the role of independent auditors need to be strengthened in almost every country.

It is not altogether surprising that the normal agencies of law enforcement usually find themselves unable to curb, let alone eliminate, corruption. Because of this governments have set up special bodies charged with the task of investigation and enforcing anti-corruption legislation. Although sizable penalties and more independent powers of inquiry are obviously helpful, it is difficult to establish any relationship between the existence of special organisations and the extent of corruption. It does not need emphasising that these agencies invariably run the risk of concentrating on the more blatant forms of monetary occupation and rarely investigate its more subtle forms. Related to this area is the whole subject of establishing a legitimate basis for "whistle-blowing".

Power and Corruption

Corruption tends to be most frequent where governments take on greater powers to bestow special privileges on various sectors of the economy and society. Where there is this concentration of power there is an urgent needs to ensure more open accountability. The media is frequently the key to this process of accountability but, unfortunately, it is often either controlled by the authorities, or subject to its own internal pressures from advertisers or other influences. Corruption is the universal disease of the body politic; it varies only in degree and visibility. It is least in extent when the press is free and uncorrupted and when the public are organised sufficiently to demand honest government. It is usually most widespread when the opposite conditions apply. But how often are cases revealed as a result of penetrating investigative journalism, rather than vulture like exposure once the revelation has come to light? And how often do unethical practices come to light from the systematic application of the control machinery, rather than almost by a accident?

Nevertheless, in essence, the problem of corruption is easily solved. If everyone worked on the assumption that whatever they did to influence a decision would be public knowledge, the vast majority of monetary and non-monetary corrupt practices would never arise.

Recent revelations suggest there are signs we are moving away from that utopian state. Yet, if this trend is not controlled and reversed, the consequences for individuals, companies will continue to be extremely serious. It can even lead to a crisis of confidence in the system itself.

For all these reasons it is not surprising to find that Ethics is now one of the most rapidly expanding subject areas everywhere.

30

Social Summit

The issues which the World Summit for Social Development is called upon to tackle—poverty, unemployment and social exclusion—are among the most critical of our time. In spite of the considerable material gains that have been registered during the past 50 years, in spite of the tremendous technological progress that has been achieved, in spite of the more favourable international political climate resulting from the end of the Cold War, poverty continues to grow and inequalities continue to widen.

Over a billion people are living in poverty. Some 30 per cent of the world's labour force is not productively employed. Many societies are being torn apart by racial, ethnic and religious conflict and intolerance. These social issues constitute the greatest threat to peace, stability and prosperity in today's world and need to be tackled with urgency and determination by policy-makers at the highest level.

If the Social Summit is to leave its mark on history, it will have to be more than a ritual gathering of Heads of State and Government. It will have to result in a perceptible improvement in the social situation in countries throughout the world—in the short and medium term, not in some indefinite future.

It will have to acknowledge that these are truly global problems which require global action in a world characterized by growing inter-dependence. National action, important though it is, will no longer suffice.

A collective commitment by all the nations of the world to the goal of full, productive and freely chosen employment is of crucial importance to the work of the Summit. It is only through their labour that individuals can contribute to the creation of wealth for their benefit and for society as a whole, can lift themselves out of poverty, can be integrated into social, economic, political and cultural life.

In view of the growing globalisation of the economy—characterized by freer trade and capital movements and greater exposure to world market forces—no country acting alone can achieve full employment without a favourable international economic environment. But we also expect emphasis to be laid on appropriate national strategies: macro-economic policies, industrial and agricultural policies which favour the growth of job-creating enterprises, education and training policies, active labour market policies which enable individuals and enterprises to adjust rapidly to changing market conditions, and policies which grant all citizens equal access to employment, education and training.

We expect the Summit to commit all nations to take special action to improve the employment prospects of those who are in a particularly disadvantaged position in the labour market—young people, disabled people, ethnic minorities. We expect it to recognize the special contribution made by women to the general welfare—through their role in the family and in production—and to end the pervasive discrimination and inequality still suffered by women.

We expect the Summit to emphasize that full employment does not mean the creation of any sort of jobs, but of high-quality jobs. We expect it to recognize the basic rights of workers—freedom of association and collective bargaining, freedom from forced labour, equal pay for work of equal value, equality of opportunity in employment and occupation.

We expect it to recognize the importance of measures which provide social security and minimum wages, which protect against arbitrary dismissal and which ensure occupational safety and health.

However balance has to be struck between the need for adequate protection and incomes on the one hand and need not to price workers and enterprises out of the market on the other. Realistic and socially acceptable solutions can only be found if those most directly concerned—employers and workers—are fully involved in decision-making on these matters through organisations of their own choosing.

Finally, and perhaps most important of all, we expect the Summit to determine the institutional framework and mechanisms for following up its conclusions. There is no point in adopting fine-sounding commitments and policies if there is no means of ensuring and monitoring follow-up action.

If the Summit fails to establish such a framework, its conclusions could well prove to be a hollow text that will quickly be forgotten.

31

Trade and Labour Standards

Using the Wrong Instruments for the Right Cause

A moral value is a shared concern of humanity; hence its enforcement should be a cooperative task implemented for the benefit of humankind. Would we qualify recent approaches to the issue of trade and labour standards as non-inquisitory but shared and cooperatives ones? The purpose of this brief is to shed some light on this question.

In fact, nobody, will deny any country the right to raise and fight for issues which are of moral concern for humanity, as they are supposed to benefit humankind. The issue of implementing and enforcing a core of labour standards one of these.

However, a problem remains: who has the negotiating power to raise and impose them? The key issue is that trade coercive attempts by some become inquisitorial as soon as they are backed by moral concerns which are supposed to be shared by all while the same "all" lack the negotiating power to be, in turn, coercive if they so wish. In other words, trade related coercion forcedly becomes "inquisition" when moral concerns are introduced into the functioning of an international trading system characterized by large imbalances in the negotiating power of the participating countries. Only a few Governments have the negotiating leverage and strength to develop what we may qualify as "trade-related inquisitory practices".

The issue of trade and labour standards seems to have arisen when "uniform competition" has been regarded as a threat to employment and economic growth in some industrial countries.

However, without attaining a certain degree of international agreement and coherence as to whether and under what conditions—a given competitive advantage is, or is not, related to social or other conditions, and whether or not it may, be considered as "unfair". With protectionist view in mind, such an approach may only be interpreted as "unbening thinking" coming from "unfair competitiveness seekers".

If the motivation behind the introduction and further use of moral argumentation is to seek a justification for the possible of trade measures as enforcement mechanisms to achieve certain goals. Particularly for harmonisation of labour standards, one may wonder why the labour standards issue has not been linked to North-North trade in the current debate on the considerable variation in labour standards among developed countries. The motivation may well be that in the post-Uruguay Round era, when tariffs have been reduced substantially and "grey area measures" put under stricter control or even banned, we may be facing the possible revival of new forms of protectionism wearing "blue", "green" or "multicolour" masks. On the contrary, if the motivation behind the introduction of such moral labour rights argumentation reflects a real commitment by the international community to enforce labour standards, a door may be open for embarking, in the future, on a series on international initiatives, not necessarily under the trade umbrella.

It should also be stressed that the linkage between trade and labour standards has been seriously misinterpreted. Most analysts remain blind to the two-way character of the link between trade and labour standards. On the one hand, trade liberalisation is to promote growth and development by promoting a more efficient allocation of resources and to ease the adoption and implementation of labour standards, as well as to promote job creation. On the other hand—and this is extremely important—raising labour standards—not keeping them low—should increasingly be seen as the real source of competitiveness and economic growth through, among others, increase in the quality of labour. There is a case for considering economic progress and the rise in labour standards as mutually reinforcing.

Turning to the low labour standard debate, much more empirical and analytical evidence is needed to asses the extent to which low labour standards are correlated to lower wages and labour costs. Although raising labour standards may not primarily be intended to maximize efficiency, it is becoming increasingly evident that efficiency and the future potential of the firm may not necessarily be maximized by keeping labour standards low. In this context, it is the development to human capital in LDCs which is a top priority, not because failing to respect labour standards in these economies threatens the welfare of the workers in the industrialized countries but, more simply, because it is the only strategy for enhancing the productivity of labour and ultimately increasing the people's standard of living. Thus, if raising labour standards and ensuring their effective implementation is important for economic progress, developed and developing countries, as well as wokers and employers in each region, should adopt a cooperative, not confrontational, approach in order to deal with this urgent and pressing problem. For this very reason, adherence to trade sanctions would be a wrong approach. Trade is essential for enhancing woker's productivity because it ensures that a country's resources will be employed in the activities that it is best at. In turn, increased productivity is the key to development, higher labour standards and higher wages. Moreover, the issue of labour standards is of a moral nature: it has an undeniable development dimension which needs to be more clearly perceived but, as discussed, it is certainly not an issue to be dealt with through trade measures.

Labour standards should be dealt with in the WTO. The capacities of the ILO will prove invaluable for renewed multilateral effort to improve working conditions in developing countries. Its tripartite structure has proved to be the best suited to the tasks of conciliation and dialogue.

Improving the standards of living and labour standards for workers or eradicatind child labour is what matters it is the right cause for humanking, a cause to fight for, through various approaches and by using all the mechanisms at our disposal in order to ensure its success. Thus, the issue is not one of trade and labour standards, but of labour standards and economic development, an issue of a human dignity and human rights nature it is a universal issue, the solutions to which should be found by all nations, taking into account equity considerations. Each country should participate in the process, depending on its level of economic development. It is precisely because economic development, including trade, is positively correlated with the adoption and effective implementation of labour standards that solutions to low labour standards should not necessarily come from negative and coercive approaches. Solutions for universal problems must not only be efficiency-based but also equity-based. Therefore, the case is for cooperation rather than coercion and for applying positive instruments. As in the case of environmental issues, developing countries should be recipients of funds, technical cooperation and other similar forms of support when the implementation of labour standards involves an inequitable cost burden.

The initiative of "grouping" a core of existing conventions into a new global convention on core labour standards of universal value may, in view of its new and distant qualitative nature, generate strong support from the international community for its implementation. The ILO was created to promote workers' right, so the initiative could be launched under its aegis, in direct collaboration with other intergovernmental organisations dealing with social, trade and development issues in an interrelated manner.

The support to this or other similar approaches by the international community, and in particular by those developed countries that have recently shown a special and strong interest in the reinforcement and implementation of labour rights in developing countries, will be a clear sign of their degree of sincerity and their willingness to share the social concerns of universal value which seem to be of paramount interest to most of their citizens.

32

Employment and Promoting Ecology

How a Service Culture Could Put People Back to Work

We are facing two big and urgent social problems: employment and ecology. Both the unemployment of millions of people and the progressive destruction of the ecosphere are alarming. But they are linked with each other. The 'greening' of industrial products, processes and services could provide many more jobs.

Unemployment has many causes, including:

- Sluggish markets;
- Stagnating or declining purchasing power;
- Growing uncertainty about the future at all levels;
- lack of will and/or ability to innovate.

But joblessness is by far due mostly to the high efficiency of industrial machinery, which produces ever more, ever faster, with ever fewer workers.

Waste of Resources

The extremely high productive use of human labour and the extremely low productive use of resources are manifested by gigantic mountains of waste. Already today, the junked cars on scrap heaps alone would form a line that would reach to the moon. The scene is the same with discarded electrical and electronic appliances. Every year, millions of tons of ovens, washing machines, refrigerators, dishwashers, TV sets, entertainment electronics equipment and small appliances are being wasted.

If we throw away all these things after a relatively short time we are not only being wasteful and irresponsible with resources, but equally so with people's work. For with the products and materials we discard, we also dispose of the human labour they contain. It is imperative that we radically reduce the enormous turnovers of material and energy. In other words, the productivity of raw materials and energy must be markedly increased. Specifically, that means we must draw as many services as possible from one kilogram of material or 1 kWh of energy. Reducing the enormous flows of materials into the industrial system, as well as developing cycles of materials and responsibility (the manufacturer taken back and repairing and/or remanufacturing used products and materials) and the main pillars of a sustainable development that can cope with the future.

The industrialized nations must cut their consumption of raw materials by a factor of about 10 by 2050; if they are to be able to handle the challenges of the future. To achieve that reduction, innovation efforts must be directed at increasing resource productivity and/or ecological efficiency. In particular, strategies to extend the useful life of goods and intensify their use could result in reducing both the speed and volume of the flows of resources to industry.

Increasing Resource Productivity

In dealing with nature, we and industry are facing radical change. This is the transition from environmental protection (preservation of nature and health) to greater resource productivity (which at the same time means greater competitiveness). As a rule, environmental protection costs money, while higher resource productivity usually cuts manufacturing costs and/or increases a company's profitability. If the company can sell the same utility or benefits while using fewer resources, it saves twofold: in buying raw materials and on waste disposal. Thereby the rule is that goods and components cycles are more profitable than resources cycles, and that the company which is first in the market gains an additional competitive advantage in terms of a lead in knowledge and image. If a service, or benefits in the form of services, can be sold instead of products, the decoupling of company success and materials flows is even greater.

Impacts on Employment

The two social problem areas of work and ecology have to date been perceived and treated separately in politics, in industry and in our own minds. And, I believe, with little result. The link between the two must be established.

The strategies to boost resource productivity would have considerable impacts on the change in industrial structures, on handling existing product inventories, and on employment. In particular, the strategies would lead to a switch of focal point from a raw materials-intensive and use-value-related service economy. This is where another view of profitability comes in. Business management would no longer focus on value added, but on maintenance of value over longer periods based on the intrinsic value of a product. Expressed as a question, the value factor, which would move to the centre of business thinking and dealing, means: how can the utilisation value be improved and sold? How can products be made with as few raw materials and as little energy as possible and create a high benefit as pollutant-free as possible for as long as possible during their entire life-cycle?

With regard to employment, the production of long-life goods would appear at first sight to lead to a reduction in the need for work. In fact, however, the strategies to increase resources productivity have positive net employment impacts. The reason is that saving resources is based in principle on substituting energy by work, rather than the reverse as has been customary to date.

If the useful life of products is extended, that will not only preserve most of the materials and energy they contain as well as the work invested in them. The products will also require a considerable amount of mostly skilled work input. Reconditioning products is as a rule more labour-intensive than manufacturing them. So large-scale reconditioning and repair work increase the number of skilled jobs and at the same time reduces the inflows of materials and energy.

Comparing a car with a life-cycle of 20 years with two others that each have useful lives of 10 years gives a good example. The first car causes an increase in employment per life-year of about 50 per cent in terms of total work input in manufacture, service, repairs and reconditioning while at the same time reducing the energy consumption by half

Regionalisation of Industry

Extending product service life would also mean replacing energy and/or capital by skilled work, helping to save money to boot. But not only rising costs of disposal, materials and energy would reduce consumption. Increasing transport costs would also mean that carrying all kinds of freight halfway around the world would make less and less business sense. That would result in ever more products and materials being circulated, reconditioned, and recycled or reduced on a regional basis. In turn, that would create regional jobs, and be more profitable as well as more promotive of technology—not only from ecological aspects.

In addition, a way of doing business which encompassed material and responsibility cycles would no longer differentiate between manufacturing and reconditioning, or between marketing and remarketing. The structure of such an economy would be predominantly decentralised and regionalised so that it could adapt itself to the new cycles. It also would benefit from the greater efficiency of the new working practices.

True, jobs would be lost in the sectors of central production, and raw materials extraction and processing. But at the same time, more and higher-skilled jobs would emerge. These would not only be better qualified jobs, but also decentralized because reconditioning, repairs and maintenance must be done near the customer. And that, in turn, would also reduce goods traffic.

In addition, skilled workers would be needed because in many cases of small production runs it makes sense and is also more economical to hire such people. They can work faster and more flexibly—and mostly cheaper—than fully-automated production lines.

There also would be a growing need for maintenance, repairs and reconditioning. More and more people would be wanted for reconditioning, that is, the remanufacturing of old products. As reconditioning involves far more craft work than highly rationalised new production, there would be a positive impact on the labour market if there were more of the former and correspondingly less of the latter.

From Production to Services

Switching to long-life products and changing from selling products to selling use-values would strengthen the current trend of jobs shifting from industrial production to the service sector. For example, if the service of individual transport were to be sold instead of the product car, the company with the competitive advantage would be the one that had a service centre in every town and village, with appropriately staffed workshops and sales or rental facilities.

Enduring change towards a knowledge-intensive and use-value-related service economy would not only mean that more people would be needed to fill jobs. It would offer more opportunities for part-time work, as well as possibilities of employment for older people and the handicapped. People who earlier could not keep up with the pace of working life would be more inclined to return to it. Another impact would be that many companies would reduce their dependence on the world market. They would no longer switch certain tasks abroad, but assign them to their part-time employees, helping them to meet their commitments as self-employed entrepreneurs.

The latter would be accommodated by an ecology-driven fiscal reform which would make massive cuts or changes in subsidies and raise the cost of energy and raw materials consumption. This move would be accompanied by a reduction in income tax and non-wage costs such as social security contributions. The market would thus be more efficient, energy- and material-intensive new production more expensive, labour-intensive repair work and reconditioning cheaper, and jobs would remain in the home country or region.

A number of more recent studies show clearly that an ecological tax reform would help to create jobs, and thereby could make a decisive contribution to reducing unemployment.

Bibliography

Agarwal, Bina. 1992. "Gender Relations and Food Security: Coping with Seasonality, Drought and Famine in South Asia." In Lourdes Benería and Shelley Feldman (eds.), *Unequal Burden: Economic Crises, Persistent Poverty, and Women's Work*. Boulder, Colo.: Westview Press.

Agarwal, Bina. 1997. "Bargaining and Gender Relations: Within and Beyond the Household." *Feminist Economics* 3(1): 1-51.

Akerlof, George A., and Rachel E. Kranton. 1999. *Economics and Identity*. Washington, D.C.: Brookings Institute.

Alkire, Sabina. 1999. "Operationalizing Amartya Sen's Capability Approach to Human Development: A Framework for Identifying 'Valuable' Capabilities," Ph.D. diss., Oxford University.

Baulch, Bob., 1996a. "Neglected Trade-Offs in Poverty Measurement." *IDS Bulletin* 27(1): 36-42.

Baulch, Bob., 1996b. "The New Poverty Agenda: A Disputed Consensus." *IDS Bulletin* 27(1): 1-10.

Bebbington A., and T. Perreault. 1999. "Social Capital, Development and Access to Resources in Highland Ecuador." *Economic Geography*. October.

Benería, Lourdes. 1989. "Gender and the Global Economy." In Arthur MacEwan and William Tabb, eds., *Instability and Change in the Global Economy*. New York: Monthly Review Press.

Berelson, Bernard. 1954. "Content Analysis." *Handbook of Social Psychology*. Vol. 1. Reading, Mass.: Addison-Wesley.

Bhatt, Mihir. 1999. "Natural Disasters as National Shocks to the Poor and Development." Disaster Mitigation Institute, Ahmedabad, India.

Booth, David, Jeremy Holland, Jesko Hentschel, Peter Lanjouw, and Alicia Herbert. 1998. *Participation and Combined Methods in African Poverty Assessment: Renewing the Agenda*. Department for International Development (DFID), U.K.: Social Development Division and Africa Division.

Bradley, Christine. 1994. "Why Male Violence against Women is a Development Issue: Reflections from Papua New Guinea." In Miranda Davies, ed., *Women and Violence: Realities and Responses, Worldwide*. London: Zed Books.

Brunetti, Aymo, Gregory Kisunko, and Beatrice Weder. 1997. "Institutions in Transition: Reliability of Rules and Economic Performance in Former Socialist Countries." Policy Research Working Paper 1809. Washington, D.C.: World Bank.

Carvalho, Soniya, and Howard White. 1997. "Combining the Quantitative and Qualitative Approaches to Poverty Measurement and Analysis: The Practice and the Potential." Technical Paper 366. Washington, D.C.: World Bank.

Castellas, Manuel. 1997. *The Power of Identity*. Malden, Mass.: Blackwell Publishers.

Cernea, Michael. 1979. "Entry Points for Sociological Knowledge in the Project Cycle." Agricultural and Rural Development Department. Washington, D.C.: World Bank.

Cernea, Michael. ed., 1985. *Putting People First*. New York: Oxford University Press.

Cernea, Michael with the assistance of April Adams. 1994. "Sociology, Anthropology and Development: An Annotated Bibliography of World Bank Publications 1975-1993." Environmentally and Sustainable Development Studies and Monograph Series 3. Washington, D.C.: World Bank.

Cernea, Michael, and Ayse Kudat. 1997. "Social Assessments for Better Development: Case Studies in Russia and

Central Asia." Environmentally Sustainable Development Studies and Monograph Series 16. Washington, D.C.: World Bank.

Chambers, Robert. 1989. "Editorial Introduction: Vulnerability, Coping and Policy." *IDS Bulletin* 20: 1.

Chambers, Robert. 1994. "The Origins and Practice of Participatory Rural Appraisal." *World Development* 22(7). Washington, D.C.: World Bank.

Chambers, Robert. 1997. "Whose Reality Counts? Putting the First Last." London: Intermediate Technology Publications.

Chambliss, William J. 1999. *Power, Politics, and Crime.* Boulder, Colo.: Westview Press.

Charmes, Jacques. 1998. "Informal Sector, Poverty and Gender: A Review of Empirical Evidence." Contributed paper for *World Development Report 2000.* Washington, D.C.: World Bank, October.

Dahle, Cheryl. 1999. "Social Justice—Alan Khazei and Vanessa Kirsch." Fast Company, Issue 30, December 1999, www. fastcompany.com.

Dasgupta, Partha, and Ismail Serageldin. 1999. *Social Capital: A Multifaceted Perspective.* Washington, D.C.: World Bank.

Davies, Miranda. ed., 1994. *Women and Violence: Realities and Responses Worldwide.* London: Zed Books.

Dollar, David, and Roberta Gatti. 1995. "Gender Inequality, Income, and Growth: Are Good Times Good for Women?" Policy Research Report on Gender and Development, No. 1. Wahington, D.C.: World Bank.

Economist Intelligence Unit. 1997. *Armenia Country Profile, 1996-97.* London: The Economist Intelligence Unit, Ltd.

Edwards, Michael, and David Hulme, eds., 1992. *Making a Difference: NGOs and Development in a Changing World.* London: Earthscan Publications.

Edwards, Robert, and Michael W. Foley. 1997. "Social Capital and the Political Economy of Our Discontent." *American Behavioural Scientist,* 40(5): 669-78.

Esman, Milton J., and Norman Uphoff. 1984. *Local Organisations: Intermediaries in Rural Development.* Ithaca, N.Y.: Cornell University Press.

Fajnzylber, Pablo, David Lederman, and Norman Loayza. 1998. *What Causes Violent Crime?* Office of the Chief Economist, Latin America and the Caribbean Region. Washington, D.C.: World Bank.

Floro, Maria Sagrario. 1995. "Economic Restructuring, Gender and the Allocation of Time." *World Development* 23: 1913-29. Washington, D.C.: World Bank.

Folbre, Nancy. 1991. "Women on Their Own: Global Patterns of Female Headship." In Rita S. Gallin, Anne Ferguson, and Janice Harper, eds., *The Women and International Development Annual.* Vol. 4. Boulder, Colo.: Westview Press.

Foley, Michael W., and Robert Edwards. 1996. "The Paradox of Civil Society." *Journal of Democracy* 7(3): 38-52.

Foster, James, and Amartya Sen. 1997. "On Economic Inequality after a Quarter Century." 2nd ed. Oxford: Clarendon Press.

Fox, Jonathan. 1993. *The Politics of Food in Mexico: State Power and Social Mobilisation.* Ithaca: Cornell University Press.

Galtung, Johan. 1994. *Human Rights in Another Key.* Cambridge, U.K.: Polity Press.

Gelles, Richard J., and Murray Straus 1998. *Intimate Violence.* New York: Simon and Schuster.

Giddens, Anthony. 1984. *The Constitution of Society.* Oxford: Blackwell.

Goetz, Anne Marie. 1998. "Women in Politics and Gender Equity on Policy: South Africa and Uganda." *Review of African Political Economy* 76: 241-62.

Greeley, Martin. 1994. "Measurement of Poverty and Poverty of Measurment." *IDS Bulletin 25*(2).

Grootaert, Christiaan. 1998. "Social Capital: The Missing Link?" Social Capital Initiative Working Paper No. 3. Social Development Family. Washington, D.C.: World Bank.

Grootaert, Christiaan. 1999. "Social Capital, Household Welfare, and Poverty in Indonesia." Policy Research Working Paper 2148. Social Development Family., Washington, D.C.: World Bank.

Grootaert, Christiaan, and Deepa Narayan. 1999. "Local Institutions, Poverty and Household Welfare in Bolivia." Social Development Family. Environmentally and Socially Sustainable Development Network. Washington, D.C.: World Bank.

Holland, Jeremy, and James Blackburn, eds., 1998. *Whose Voice? Participatory Research and Policy Change.* London: Intermediate Technology Publications.

Hyden, Goran. 1997. "Civil, Society, Social Capital, and Development: Dissection of a Complex Discourse." *Studies in Comparative International Development* 32: 3-30.

Jackson, Cecile. 1996. "Rescuing Gender from the Poverty Trap." *World Development* 23:489-504.

Jain, Devaki. 1996. "Panchayat Raj: Women Changing Governance." Gender in Development Programme. United Nations Development Programme, New York.

Kabeer, Naila. 1997. "Women, Wages and Intra-household Power Relations in Urban Bangladesh." *Development and Change* 28(2): 261-302.

Kabeer, Naila, and Ramya Subrahmanian. 1996. *Institutions, Relations and Outcomes: Framework and Tools for Gender-aware Planning*. University of Sussex; U.K.: Institute of Development Studies.

Kaufmann, Georgia. 1997. "Watching the Developers: A Partial Ethnography." In R.D. Grillo and R.L. Stirrat, eds., *Discourses of Development: Anthropological Perspectives.* Oxford: Berg Press.

Korten, David C. 1990. *Getting to the 21st Century: Voluntary Action and the Global Agenda.* West Hartford, Conn.: Kumarian Press.

Krishna, Anirudh, and Norman Uphoff. 1999. "Mapping and Measuring Social Capital: A Conceptual and Empirical Study of Collective Action for Conserving and Developing Watersheds in Rajasthan, India." Social Capital Initiative Working Paper No. 13. Washington, D.C.: World Bank.

Krishan, Anirudh, Norman Uphoff, and Milton J. Esman (eds.), 1997. *Reason for Hope: Instructive Experiences in Rural Development.* West Hartford, Conn.: Kumarian Press.

Leach, Melissa, Robin Mearns, and Ian Scoones. 1997. *Community-Based Sustainable Development: Consensus or Conflict?* University of Sussex, U.K.: Institute of Development Studies.

Lipton, Michael, and Martin Ravallion. 1995. "Poverty and Policy." In Jere Richard Behrman and Thirukodikaval Nilakanta Srinivasan, eds. *Handbook of Development Economics.* Vol. 3. Amsterdam: Elsevier Press.

MacEwen Scott, Alison. 1995. "Informal Sector or Female Sector? Gender Bias in Urban Labour Maket Models." In Diane Elson, ed., *Male Bias in the Development Process.* 2nd ed. Manchester, U.K.: Manchester University Press.

Marshall, Gordon. 1994. *The Concise Oxford Dictionary of Sociology.* New York: Oxford University Press.

Max-Neef, Manfred. 1993. *Human Scale Development: Conception, Application, and Further Reflections.* London: Apex Press.

Milanovic, Branko. 1998. *Income, Inequality, and Poverty During the Transition from Planned to Market Economy.* Regional and Sectoral Studies. Washington, D.C.: World Bank.

Milimo, John T. 1995. "An Analysis of Qualitative Information on Agriculture: from Beneficiary Assessments, Participatory Poverty Assessments and Other Studies which used Qualitative Research Methods." Ministry of Agriculture, Food, and Fisheries. Lusaka, Zambia

Moore, Mick, and James Putzel. "Thinking Strategically about Politics and Poverty." IDS Working Paper 101. University of Sussex, U.K.: Institute of Development Studies.

Moser, Caroline. 1998. *The Asset-Vulnerability Framework: Reassessing Urban Poverty Reduction Strategies.* Washington, D.C.: World Bank.

Moser, Caroline, Annika Tornqvist, and Bernice van Bronkhorst. 1998. "Mainstreaming Gender and Development in the World Bank: Progess and Recommendations." Washington, D.C.: World Bank.

Narayan, Deepa. 1999. "Bonds and Bridges: Social Capital and Poverty." Policy Research Working Paper 2167. Policy Research Department. Washington, D.C.: World Bank.

Narayan, Deepa, and Katrinka Ebbe. 1997. "Design of Social Funds: Participation, Demand Orientation, and Local Organisational Capacity." Discussion Paper No. 375. Washington, D.C.: World Bank.

Narayan, Deepa, and Lant Pritchett. 1999. "Cents and Sociability: Household Income and Social Capital in Rual Tanzania." *Economic Development and Cultural Change* (47)4: 871-878.

Narayan, Deepa, and Lyra Srinivasan. 1994. *Participatory Development Tool Kit: Training Materials for Agencies and Communities* Washington, D.C.: World Bank.

Narayan, Deepa and Michael Cassidy. 1999. "A Dimensional Approach to Measuring Social Capital: Development and Validation of a Social Capital Inventory." Draft. Washington, D.C.: World Bank.

Narayan, Deepa, and Talat Shah. 2000. *Gender Inequity, Poverty, and Social Capital.* Policy Research Report on Gender Development, Working Paper Series. Washington, D.C.: World Bank.

North, Douglas. 1990. "Institutions and their Consequences for Economic Performance." In Karen Schweers Cook and Margaret Levi, eds., *The Limits of Rationality*. Chicago, Ill.: University of Chicago.

Norton Andy, and Thomas Stephens. 1995. "Participation in Poverty Assessments." Social Development Paper 9. Washington, D.C.: World Bank.

Orbach, Susie. 1999. "Psychoanalysis and Social Policy." Seminar Paper Presented to the World Bank, Washington, D.C.: April.

Patton, Michael Quinn. 1990. *Qualitative Evaluation and Research Methods*. Newbury Park, Calif.: Sage Publications.

Portes, Alejandro. 1998. "Social Capital: Its Origins and Applications in Modern Sociology." *Annual Review of Sociology* 22: 1-24.

Pottier, Johan. 1997. "Towards an Ethnography of Participatory Appriasal and Research." In R.D. Grillo and R.L. Stirrat, eds., *Discourses of Development: Anthropological Perspectives*. Oxford, U.K.: Berg Press.

Putnam Robert, Robert Leonardi, and Raffaella Y. Nanetti. 1993. *Making Democracy Work: Civic Traditions in Modern Italy*. Princeton, N.J.: Princeton University Press.

Ravallion, Martin. 1995. "China's Lagging Poor Areas." *American Economic Review, Papers and Procedures* 89: 301-5.

Ray, Raka, and Anna Kortweg. 1999. "Women's Movements in the Third World: Identity, Mobilisation and Autonomy." *Annual Review of Sociology* 25: 47-71.

Rietbergen-McCracken, Jennifer, and Deepa Narayan. 1998. "Participatory Tools and Techniques: A Resource Kit for Participation and Social Assessment" Social Policy and Resettlement Division, Environment Department. Washington, D.C.: World Bank.

Robb, Caroline. 1999. "Can the Poor Influence Poverty? Participatory Poverty Assessments in the Developing World." Washington, D.C.: World Bank.

Rodrik, Dani. 1998 "Globalisation, Social Conflict and Economic Growth." *World Economy* 21(1): 43-58.

Rupesinghe, Kumar, and Marcial Rubio. 1994 *The Culture of Violence.* New York: United Nations University Press.

Salmen, Lawrence. 1987. *Listen to the People.* New York; Oxford University Press.

Salmen, Lawrence. 1995. "Participatory Poverty Assessment: Incorporating Poor People's Perspectives into Poverty Assessment Work." Social Development Paper No. 11. Washington, D.C.: World Bank.

Salmen, Lawrence. 1998. "Toward a Listening Bank: A Review of Best Practices and the Efficacy of Beneficiary Assessment." Social Development Paper No. 23. Washington, D.C.: World Bank.

Sartori, Giovanni. 1997. "Understanding Pluralism." *Journal of Democracy* 8(4): 58-69.

Schuler, Sidney Ruth, Syed M. Hashemi, and Shamsul Huda Badal. 1998. "Men's Violence Against Women in Rural Bangladesh: Undermined or Exacerbated by Microcredit Programmes?" *Development in Practice* 8(2): 148-57.

Schwartz, S.H. 1994. "Are There Universal Aspects in the Structure and Contents of Human Values?" *Journal of Social Issues* 50(4): 19-45.

Sen, Amartya K. 1981. *Poverty and Famines.* Oxford: Clarendon Press.

Sen, Amartya K. 1983. "Poor, Relatively Speaking." *Oxford Economic Papers* 35: 153-69. Reprinted in *Resources, Values and Development.*

Sen, Amartya K. 1984. "Rights and Capabilities." In Amartya K. Sen, ed., *Resources, Values and Development.* Oxford, U.K.: Blackwell.

Sen, Amartya K. 1985. "A Sociological Approach to the Measurement of Poverty: A Reply to Professor Peter Townsend." *Oxford Economic Papers* 37: 669-76.

Sen, Amartya K. 1992. *Inequality Reexamined.* Cambridge, Mass: Harvard University Press.

Sen, Amartya K. 1993. "Economic Regress: Concepts and Features." *Proceedings of the World Bank Annual Conference on Development Economics,* 315-54.

Sen, Amartya K. 1997. *On Economic Inequlity.* 2nd ed. Oxford: Clarendon Press.

Sen, Amartya K. 1999. *Development as Freedom.* New York: Knopf Press.

Shah, Shekhar. 1999. "Coping with Natural Disasters: The 1998 Floods in Bangladesh." Seminar paper presented in June to the World Bank, Washington, D.C.

Shapiro, Gilbert, and John Markoff. 1997. "A Matter of Definition." In Carl W. Roberts, ed., *Text Analysis for the Social Sciences.* Mahwah, N.J.: Lawrence Erlbaum Assoicates.

Silverman, David. 1993. *Interpreting Qualitative Data: Methods for Analyzing Talk, Text and Interaction.* Thousand Oaks, Calif.: Sage Publications.

Srinivas, Smita. 1999. *Social Protection for Women Workers in the Informal Economy.* Draft. Washington, D.C.: World Bank and Geneva; International Labour Office.

Standing, Guy. 1999. "Global Feminisation through Flexible Labour: A Theme Revisited." *World Development* 3(27): 583-602.

Stone, P.J., D.C. Dunphy, M.S. Smith, and D.M. Ogilvie. 1966. *The General Inquirer: A Computer Approach to Content Analysis.* Cambridge: MIT Press.

Strauss, Anselm. 1987. *Qualitative Analysis for Social Scientists.* New York: Cambridge University Press.

Tarrow, Sidney. 1994. *Power in Movement: Social Movements, Collective Action and Politics.* Cambridge, U.K.: Cambridge University Press.

Tendler, Judith. 1997. *Good Government in the Tropics. Baltimore,* Md.: Johns Hopkins University Press.

Townsend, Peter. 1971. *The Concept of Poverty.* London: Heinemann Educational.

Tripp, Aili Mari. 1992. "The Impact of Crisis and Economic Reform on Women in Urban Tanzania." In Lourdes Benerla and Shelly Feldman (eds.), *Unequal Burden: Economic Crises, Persistent Poverty, and Women's Work.* Boulder, Colo.: Westview Press.

Uphoff, Norman. 1986. *Local Institutional Development: An Analytical Sourcebook with Cases.* West Hartford, Conn.: Kumarian Press.

Uphoff, Norman, Milton J. Esman, and Anirudh Krishna. 1997. *Reasons for Success: Learning from Instructive Experiences in Rural Development.* West Hartford, Conn.: Kumarian Press.

Visaria, Leela. 1999. "Violence Against Women in India: Evidence from Rural Gujarat." In *Domestic Violence in India: A Summary Report of Three Studies.* Washington, D.C.: International Center for Research on Women.

Weber, Robert Philip. 1990. *Basic Content Analysis.* 2nd ed. Newbury Park, Calif.: Sage Publications.

WHO (World Health Organisation). 1997. *Violence Against Women.* Geneva.

Woolcock, Michael. 1998. "Social Capital and Economic Development: Toward a Theoretical Synthesis and Policy Framework." *Theory and Society* 27(2): 151-208.

Woolcock, Michael, and Deepa Narayan. 2000. "Social Capital: Implications for Development Theory, Research, and Policy." *World Bank Research Observer* 15(2), Washington, D.C.: World Bank.

World Bank. 1996a. *From Plan to Market: World Development Report 1996.* Washington, D.C.

World Bank. 1996b. *Sourcebook on Participation.* Washington, D.C.

World Bank. 1997a. *Poverty Assessment: A Process Review.* Operations Evaluation Department Document 15881. Washington, D.C.

World Bank. 1997b. *World Development Report 1997: The State in a Changing World.* New York: Oxford University Press (for the World Bank).

World Bank. 1998. *World Development Indicators.* Washington, D.C.

World Bank. 1999. *World Development Indicators.* Washington, D.C.

World Bank. 2000. *Poverty Trends and Voices of the Poor.* Poverty Reduction Group. Washington, D.C.

Wratten, Ellen, 1995. "Conceptualizing Urban Poverty." *Environment and Urbanisation* 7: 11-36.

Index

D

E